FOR DIY-INDIES

SONGWRITERS. PUBLISHERS. ARTISTS. LABELS.

INCLUDES: PRACTICAL TIPS, HINTS, and HOW-TO's FRIENDLY to DIY/INDIES, PLUS WATCHLISTS of TRAPS AND TRICKS TO AVOID.

MUSIC BUSINESS SURVIVAL MANUAL

FROM DIY/INDIE HQ: DURDEN'S DOWN & DIRTY DISPATCHES.

by ANGELA K. DURDEN
Author of *Navigating the New Music Business as a DIY/Indie*

Foreword by David LaMotte
Author of *Worldchanging 101: Challenging the Myth of Powerlessness*

Special sections from DIY/Indies	Ken Bonfield	Tony Wasilewski
	Lance Allen	Marc Jackson

MUSIC BUSINESS SURVIVAL MANUAL
IMPRINT: SECOND BIGHT PUBLISHING
DECATUR, GEORGIA 30033

The "**Music Business Survival Manual**" is designed to first teach necessary concepts and techniques — and point to tools and methods — that are working for other successful DIY/Indies.

It will also point out traps and roadblocks to your ability to have something good to show for your hard work.

This book includes some evergreen content originally included in the 2015 book *Navigating the New Music Business as a DIY & Indie*.

The importance of survival in the wilds of the music business is paramount for those who want to make a profit from their talent. This follow-up book goes deeper into the threats to the DIY/Indie's ability to keep their business strong and thus giving it the opportunity to thrive.

This book is **the** authoritative, straightforward, clear, and simple guide full of real-world advice for all **Indie** songwriters, composers, artists, publishers, bands, and labels whose vocation requires being familiar with the music business landscape.

Being surprised in business can kill a career. Therefore, prepare. Do not forsake important tasks because they are boring. These are what will allow you to follow your passion, support yourself and your family — and have the life you want.

Sustainable Career

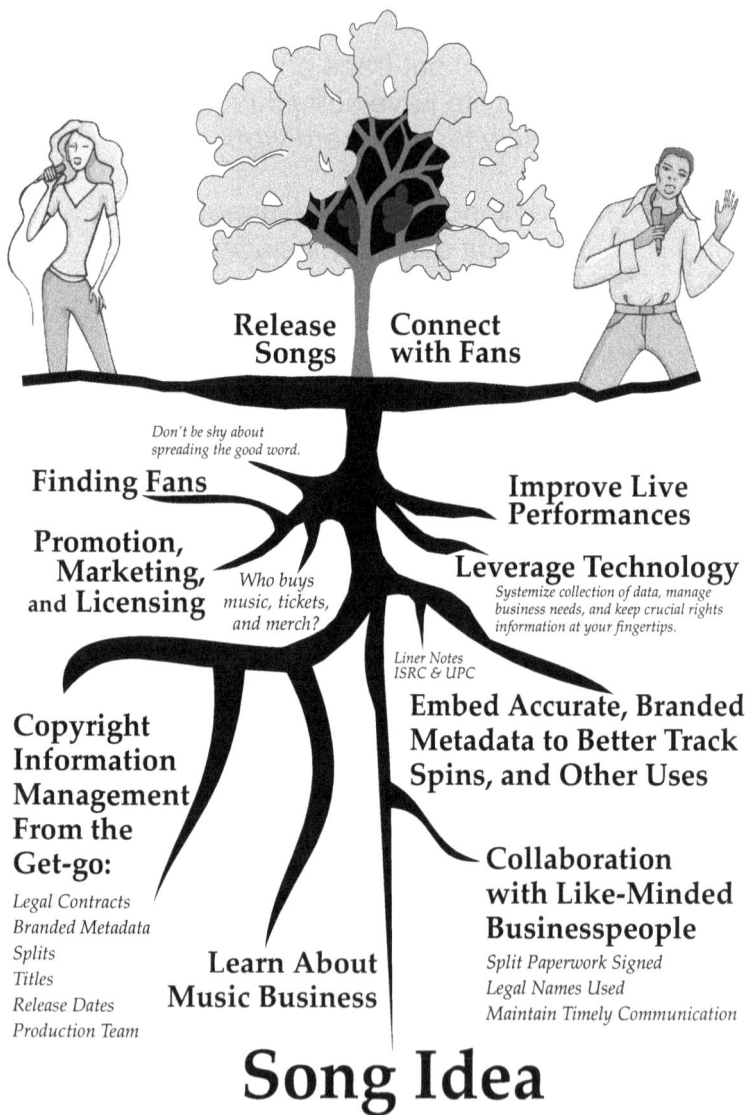

Release Songs

Connect with Fans

Don't be shy about spreading the good word.

Finding Fans

Promotion, Marketing, and Licensing

Who buys music, tickets, and merch?

Improve Live Performances

Leverage Technology
Systemize collection of data, manage business needs, and keep crucial rights information at your fingertips.

Liner Notes
ISRC & UPC

Copyright Information Management From the Get-go:

Legal Contracts
Branded Metadata
Splits
Titles
Release Dates
Production Team

Embed Accurate, Branded Metadata to Better Track Spins, and Other Uses

Collaboration with Like-Minded Businesspeople

Split Paperwork Signed
Legal Names Used
Maintain Timely Communication

Learn About Music Business

Song Idea

KEN BONFIELD SAYS: The way to succeed in the music business is to stay in the music business.

SURVIVAL

"Godmother and wand."
Only in fairy tales
do they deliver
what you want.

Failing is
success if in
the failing you
identify what
did not work.

SECTIONS
OF THE BOOK

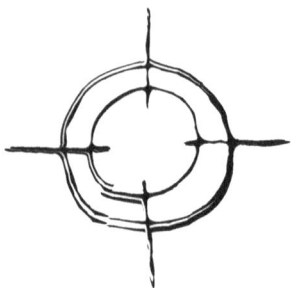

TARGET.

Good for your
DIY/Indie business.
Ignore at your peril.

15-56

BE AWARE.

You may interact with these
things at some point, so plan
how to deal with them when
they come up.

75-89

DANGER!

Can sink your small business
and ruin future chances and
careers. Good to know about,
though; there are plenty
who will push you toward
these because it supports
their business model.

105-108

DURDEN'S
DOWN & DIRTY
DISPATCHES

119-201

QUICK-FIND

FOREWORD

David LaMotte
Musician and Author
DavidLaMotte.com

The power of a dream acted upon.

I've been a professional independent musician for nearly thirty years. That translates to twelve Indie albums, and over three thousand concerts on five continents. I've stood on stages next to some of my heroes, and had the extraordinary privilege of writing and sharing songs as my job.

It's also true that the majority of people in my state, in my country, and in the world have never heard of me — and probably never will. That's what a successful independent music career looks like.

It's about finding the small but devoted group who will be passionate about what you do, and honoring the relationships formed through your music.

You make music because you must. Because music matters. Because music is part of the definition of being alive for you.

Then, to honor your music and the people who listen to it, you do the drudgery of booking, publicity, bookkeeping, etc., or you make sure it gets done because it must.

And if you do both pieces — the art and the business — with persistence and conscious attention to your goals and your plans for achieving them, you have a career.

The first workshop I ever taught was called Creativity and Practical Dream Following. It addressed this question:

How does one get from being a passionate unknown artist to having a sustainable career?

That *practical* part is the rub for many musicians. We know how to create art, but we don't always know how to work on the other part — the business of being self-employed as musicians, performers, writers. Usually, at least for a while, that means being our own managers, booking agents, accountants, publicists, office staff, etc.

A successful independent music career will quickly become a small business. How do we learn to run a small business? How do we reach folks who might connect with our music, and then maintain those relationships? How do we navigate the complex, sometimes arcane, yet constantly shifting music industry?

How do we make sense of performing rights organizations, copyrights, publishing, split sheets, recording contracts, crowdfunding, digital distribution, licensing, and the endless offers from companies who dubiously promise to make those things easy and profitable for us?

Navigating the music industry is perhaps the most daunting section of the list. And it is that part Angela K. Durden has generously taken on in this book. In clear and helpful terms, Durden explains the sometimes baffling, extremely powerful, and not-so-friendly-to-independent-artists Music Industry. She not only decodes the mysterious lingo and complex relationships between different parts of the business, she also gives clear advice about hazards to avoid — and why to avoid them.

If you hope to take your music out into the world, and even have dreams of that music supporting you financially, you will need a roadmap to navigate a complex and competitive industry. Fortunately, you are already holding it in your hands.

Even if you don't want your music to be your profession, this book will provide useful advice as you seek to share it, and it will give support you need to treat your art with the respect it deserves.

To be clear, art for art's sake is worthwhile. Even if your music never leaves your living room, but you create good art there and it nourishes you, you've done something that matters. Celebrate it.

There are many ways to make music work as a profession and/or passion. Some of the best musicians I've ever known had day jobs outside of the music industry. Some folks put a lot of stock in being a "professional" musician, in the sense of paying your bills with your music; but really, isn't that a question of accounting rather than a matter of art?

The words *professional* and *amateur* are worth examining.

Your profession is that which you profess; it's what you claim. When someone asks what you do, the answer is your profession. Amateur is a French word meaning "lover of" in the sense of "one who loves" a thing. When someone asks what you love to do, you are an amateur of the thing you name when you answer.

So, in the music business especially, you can be both. In fact, if you ever stop being an amateur, you may want to stop being a professional as well. But if your love of your art is strong enough, it will make the risk and drudgery worthwhile. Take the business side of your vocation seriously. Making a living with your music allows you to spend more time doing it, and thus develop your career and your craft.

If you're already making money playing music or even making a living, you are to be congratulated! It's a tough thing to do. And it's made tougher by the fact that the playing field keeps shifting. *Those shifts mean that the timeworn models and strategies may no longer be effective.* In some cases, they definitely aren't.

Every industry goes through periods of transformation and jobs are lost. Massive and quick change is not specific to the music business.

It's also important to acknowledge that the major label model of success is seldom applicable to independent artists. When I was a young musician playing in bars, people used to encourage me by saying they couldn't wait until I was "discovered".

Those well-intentioned people were remembering a time when major labels actually sent talent scouts on the road looking for talented, undiscovered musicians whose music they could sell to the world. They didn't realize those times had passed long before.

In fact, those times were already gone long before I was getting started in the early nineties. These days, the major labels that are left are more likely to sign a lot of artists that seem fairly promising, put virtually no financial investment into them, and wait to see if some of those artists — through their own hard work — will *hit* and become sufficiently known that the label can make some money on their music.

But even in the so-called good old days of the music industry, the predominant model of success was to have a song (or more than one) top the charts by being quickly exposed to large numbers of people, though generally for a short period of time. Even now, that strategy can yield a significant windfall, and it has worked out well for a small number of people. Those who were wise enough not to expect that income to last fared even better.

On the other hand, the Indie music model has to do with developing a fan base over time and keeping in touch with them once you find each other. With notable exceptions, most professional musicians fall into one of those categories — having a large quantity of casual listeners for a short period of time or a smaller number of passionate listeners for a longer stretch.

That smaller number of people can sustain a career for decades if you continue to offer something they value.

That is doubly true if the thing you offer is hard to find elsewhere. This is what people mean when they talk about a "niche market". If the thing you bring is unusual, in whatever way, and you do it well and it matters to people, a small number of listeners will remain your devoted fans for a very long time.

As a folk singer who writes songs that require attention to the lyrics to appreciate them, I've already carved off the vast majority of music listeners who don't listen primarily to acoustic music, and certainly don't listen closely enough to consider the lyrics. Therefore, because I already know most people aren't interested in what I do, I can stay focused on those who are interested and avoid wasting effort where I get little or no return.

For those who listen closely and care deeply about music, it is a rare treasure to discover an artist they relate to. They have endured thousands of songs that get worse rather than better when they listen closely. Fans will be fiercely loyal if you honor the time, emotion, and money they have invested in you and your art by offering them the best of yourself.

As you set out to find your audience and develop your work, good mentors are indispensable, especially if you're doing this work outside of a standard music business model where industry mentors are usually found. It is wise to seek them out in person, but also in books like this one.

A good mentor will save you from making certain mistakes that can destroy your career so that you have opportunity to make other mistakes — an inevitable part of being an artist. The only way to avoid mistakes is to avoid taking chances, and you can't be a successful artist without taking chances. Still, the learning is cumulative, and a good mentor can literally save your career. This book is a great place to start. Despite nearly three decades on the road as a professional musician, I found things in this book that were new to me.

Angela K. Durden is a good guide as you travel a road with some really impressive hazards. She has written a book that decodes the web of systems and organizations that make up the music biz. In each chapter, she explains the pieces of the puzzle, makes clear recommendations, and raises flags to indicate where the potholes are, so you can avoid plunging into them.

The world really does need more good music, and yours deserves to be treated with respect, which means honoring it by sharing it and by protecting it. Music moves people, both figuratively and literally. When a sound wave travels through the air and meets your body, it goes all the way through, vibrating every cell and atom. It is an extremely powerful force.

People who don't really understand that power are likely to say your music won't change the world. Artists are often dismissed as naïve dreamers. The truth, though, is that it's not naïve to think you can change the world. It's naïve to think you could possibly be in the world and not change it. Everything you do changes the world, whether you like it or not. And when you bring intention to those changes, as you do with your art, it can have powerful effects.

Music literally saves lives. It can touch hope in hearts that have all but given in to despair. It can change hearts, which can change actions. It can offer connection across lines that are meant to divide. Its significance should not be understated.

But for it to have an effect, someone needs to hear it. The good news is that it is possible to get your music out into the world, and to be supported by the folks who love it. Dreams do come true. I know. Mine have. The other news is that it takes some study and some work to make all of that happen.

The power of a dream acted upon should not be understated either.

The world needs dreamers. Dreaming and envisioning are important steps in creating a better world. Henry David Thoreau wrote, "If you have built castles in the air, your work need not be lost. That is where they should be. Now go and build their foundations."

You have probably already built the dream.

Now it's time to start on the foundation.

David LaMotte
June 2018

SURVIVAL

The Music Business

is not the same as

the art of music.

But to make money from
the art, one must
learn and master
the basics of
the business.

THE TRUTH, DOWN & DIRTY

A friend said, "Before you can thrive, you have to survive." My friend is correct.

Therefore this book is about survival. What do you need to do first and foremost? What do you need to be aware of? What should you avoid at all costs? That's what you'll find in here.

Survival only happens if you have the *will* to make it, plan to properly use what is available around you, and have an ability to identify threats even if never seen before.

As of February 2018, the three PROs in the U.S. represented 1.48 million songwriters and publishers with 24.9 million songs in their repertories. That's a lot.

PRO	Members	Songs Represented
ASCAP	650,000	11,500,000
BMI	800,000	13,000,000
SESAC	30,000	400,000
TOTALS	1,480,000	24,900,000

Because of improvements in technology removing the expensive barrier to entry, between 1945 and 1959 the number of recording studios grew from a relative handful to almost two thousand. We hit a similar technology shift beginning in the mid 1980s and again in the mid 2000s. Extremely affordable and high-quality software and firmware have grown the number of home and small recording studios, and the ranks of the DIY/Indies, to uncountable numbers.

Also, during this time memberships began to grow in the ASCAP and BMI organizations. With those numbers you would expect the music business to be wildly successful.

That is not the case. Here's why. One thing everybody in all areas of the business has run up against is this:
Getting their music heard.

Used to be that getting on radio was a no-brainer. To make it to the top of the listening pile, entering onto the scene came the under-the-table exchange involving records and money in a straight deal of pay-to-get-played called payola.

To stop payola, radio companies formed committees to choose the music. Individual disc jockeys were no longer allowed to decide. Laws were passed against it. Stations stopped "breaking a record".

But radio missed the money stream. That led to a corporate budget line item called marketing/promotion. Labels and publishers could now buy radio exposure and it was considered a tax-deductible expense.

In all cases, who got shut out? The little guy, the do-it-your-selfer. The independent. The guy who had a dream and was going to go out and make it happen. Now the barriers to entry were several-fold. Payola: Against the law. Legally booking time: Out of reach. DJ's choice: Non-existent.

You see, now the artist could no longer drive around to the radio stations, drop off his newest single, and have an on-air chat with the DJ — many of whom had great autonomy and might play his record even without payola. And the Little

Guy could never get in front of the committees because he only represented his singular tiny interests.

More such decisions caused the music business to begin not to be so profitable overall. Sure, there were still the big hits, but there was so much that wasn't being heard. The listening public was getting bored hearing the same thing over and over, causing radios not to be turned on.

Ad revenues fell just as home systems, portable, and onboard music playing devices became popular. Eight-track and cassette tapes, then CD players made the concept of User Defined Playlists a simple reality and much welcomed by fans and music lovers.

Then along came that Wild West show called the Internet.

Controls had to be put in place there, too. (Remember Napster?) Somebody needed to handle the huge influx of music and the payments to rights holders.

Enter CD Baby and a few other select companies who would, for a reasonable fee, be able to put your music in front of the endless stream of listeners and music buyers on the Internet. Can you say *easy money?* But for whom and for how long? It became clear it certainly was not best for most creators.

The next level of fraud and predatory behavior from monopolistic hordes of raiders was so big nobody could believe it. Many digital aggregators, digital distributors, and sub-distributors set up systems that could be called wholesale theft using wink-and-nod collusion between performing rights organizations and aggregators who play fast and loose with intellectual property rights.

Or how about China? Operating a massive industry based on counterfeiting products rightfully belonging to others but that, for entire generations, has pounded away at their ability to sell a good product.

I've been shining a light in those dark places and let me tell you, I've been heard. The Bigs, The Majors, and Tech Giants as well as their handmaidens think that because I'm just one little girl, nobody listens.

But I know they are wrong because I hear from DIY/Indies all the time. They say:

"Angela, I just got through reading your book *Navigating the New Music Business as a DIY & Indie* on the music business. Wow. I understand now. Very helpful."

"Angela, thank you so much for writing that article on [fill in the article here]. I looked up all this stuff and you were right. [Company name here] is stealing from me."

"Angela, I don't like to read, but I read that book twice this weekend. I only put it down to go to the bathroom."

My 2015 book mentioned above was the first of its kind. You see, there are a lot of books on how to succeed in the music business. All you need do is search on the phrase "music business" and up pops a huge list of business books on the subject. Most of the books are written by experts — entertainment attorneys, songwriters, and artists.

Plaster *UPDATED!* on covers, and add a chapter or new intro, and the books sell all over again, proving there is a huge need for business information. You can bet, though, it isn't industry insiders buying these books.

But guess what? Those books are so out of date as to be laughable. Add to that, so much of their information is incorrect that they should be sued for selling a book under false pretenses.

The thing is, though, many of these "experts" are embedded with The Majors and The Bigs. Some have even become spokespersons for Tech Giants. This is their truth: The stories they tell of success, and their approach to the business, only support large companies with international business interests who must make quarterly profits on the backs of the *new massive slave class: The independent creative, the songwriter, and the artist.*

The problem is that the music business model has changed. And it changed so rapidly that these experts trapped themselves and are now gnawing on their own legs while continuing to mislead their DIY/Indie readers.

I wouldn't venture so far as to say that every word is untrue in those other books, though a reader has to dig through the rambling, ill-conceived, badly written, and convoluted texts to find anything useful. They are a waste of time and money. I know because I bought them, too.

I hate time-wasters and don't appreciate being duped into spending my hard-earned money.

So when I wrote *Navigating the New Music Business as a DIY & Indie* (still available on amazon.com), it was not going to be anything like what was out there. I was successful in reaching that goal. I'm proud of the book.

But this book, *Music Business Survival Guide*, is getting even more specific. Since 2015 when I wrote *Navigating,* there have been more changes affecting the DIY/Indie's ability to promote, sell, own, or otherwise profit from their music.

Changes in technology, the economy, the political situation, as well as information coming out about long-term global assaults on creatives' rights designed to cheat *you* and waged by The Majors, The Bigs, Tech Giants, and entire countries, have done two things. **One:** Made it ever more imperative for you to watch your back, watch the terrain upon which you locate your business, and keep a listen-out for the growls of hungry predators sniffing for your dollar. And, **two:** Their market approach has backed The Majors, The Bigs, and Tech Giants into a corner where they are pummeling themselves to death.

So, now we know what isn't working. We know all artists and songwriters — big and small, famous or otherwise — are getting cheated worse than ever. And this despite efforts of government, the Recording Academy, PROs, non-profits, and others to protect us. But what will work?

Simply this: Control access to your I.P. Find *your* fans. *Sell* them something. And *keep* your money in your pocket.

Now, go get 'em.

Angela K. Durden

December 2018

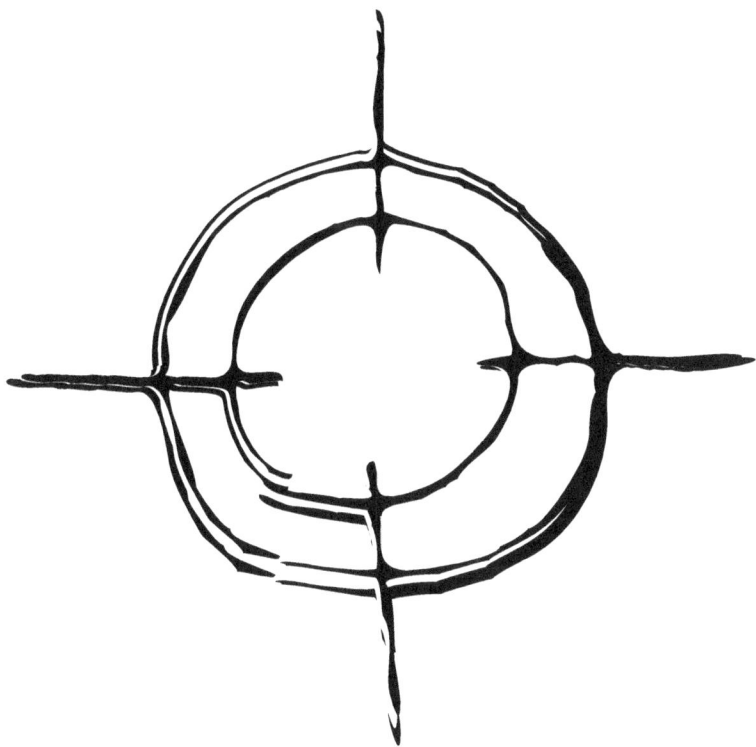

TARGET.

Good for your
DIY/Indie business.
Ignore at your peril.

CATALOG:

An organized listing of intellectual property owned or controlled by a publisher or writer, containing proofs of ownership, and rights to license as well as sell your Intellectual Property (I.P.), which means your songs. Each song should have documented:

- All titles the song goes by.
- Date written.
- Date completed song was released.
- Where the song was released.
- All writers/composers' legal names.
- All publishers' names. (These can be companies or individuals.)
- Split sheet with writer(s)/composer(s) and publisher(s) percentages agreed upon, dated, and signed by all parties to that song. (See sample split sheet on page 17 for complete information needed.)
- Work-for-hire contracts even for those who "volunteered" for no pay to help out "their good buddy", and for all musicians, singers, producers, engineers, etc. who were paid to do a task to get your song done.
- Assigned and embedded ISRC number.
- Album song is on, if it is included on an album.
- Whether or not the song includes licensed or unlicensed works by others, also known as samples.

SPLIT SHEET:

A listing of each owner of the song. Owners can be any combination of writers only, or writers and publishers, with the percentage ownership stake of each stated. Percentages cannot equal more or less than 100. **See the next page for an example of a split sheet.**

Sample Split Sheet: Does not need to look like this, but MUST have this information for each writer, composer, and publisher that is on the deal for each song.

Editor's note: In this example C/S/Z stands for City, State, and ZIP Code.
Author's note: The fewer people on the split sheet, the more negotiating room you have for placements on other artists' albums, and the higher the royalty check will be.

Song Split Sheet

Date: _____

Project: _____

Song Working Title: _____

Song Final Title: _____

Percentages (%) of agreed and assigned splits

Songwriters' Names   Affiliation

Name:	SESAC
Address:	ASCAP
	BMI
C/S/Z:	Other
email:	_____
Agreed-to signature:	COUNTRY: _____
	Songwriter: %
Other % (See additional info and notes below)	

Publishers' Names   Affiliation

Name:	SESAC
Address:	BMI
	ASCAP
C/S/Z:	Other
email:	_____
Agreed-to signature:	COUNTRY: _____
	Publishing: %
Other % (See additional info and notes below)	

Additional info and notes:

Guaranteeing exposure.

New songwriters and artists are pressured to work for what is famously called "The Exposure". There is nothing wrong with not getting any actual money for your part in a project. However, too many are equating not getting any money with **not having to document their role in the song.** For instance, like being on a split sheet for a song or being on the advertising posters for a live gig.

Exposure only matters if you can *prove* you were involved. Let's take recording. Are you on the split sheet even if the split is zero percent? Are you listed on the liner notes as having contributed something specific? Are you only getting a generic thank you — or no mention at all?

Having no paperwork means minimal or no bragging rights for you. Not being able to take credit for your contribution — of lyrics, hooks, vocals, instrumentation, production, mixing, engineering, etc. — only means that your reputation is harmed as you go around saying, "I was on that song, they just didn't list me."

One can say they were "in the room" or "wrote the hook" or "came up with the melody line".

But if the documenting system — deal paperwork, listing with performing rights organizations, metadata, and so forth — does not know you exist, then everybody just thinks you're lying.

Then you get mad because not only did you not make any money, you've got nothing to show for your effort. I wish I could say this is atypical, but it isn't. Happens all the time.

Artists say, "You know what. Enough of this. I'm going to put out an album of my own. I'm going to own all the publishing and writing shares and get all the money."

Then they release their album, and yet have still not documented they own it. No metadata is embedded that shows they are the rights owner — that is, the writer and/or publisher and/or label. They haven't set themselves up as a publisher with their PRO. Then they basically give their music away to digital distributors.

They don't follow up with anything.

The stories are endless of how people have lost control of their intellectual property. Let me tell you about "Kevin," a real man I know.

In 2014, Kevin wrote, recorded, listed with BMI, and released over 15 original works and included these on one album. Kevin registered each song's copyright with Copyright.gov. He also used CD Baby Pro to distribute the album. Kevin received royalty checks from BMI and CD Baby through first quarter of 2016. He has received nothing since from either BMI or CD Baby.

Kevin sat in front of me with his laptop. I asked him if he was a publisher; he said he *thought* he was. Easy enough to find out, I told him, look at your BMI member portal. He logged in, clicked his catalog hyperlink, then he clicked the first song on the list. Who was listed as publisher? CD Baby Alpha Music. Kevin was quite upset. His BMI payouts were only for writer/composer.

All that money left on the table. Kevin thought registering copyright meant he got all the money. But Kevin didn't understand how the money flows. Just because one may register a song's copyright does not mean one can collect all the money for its use.

It's very sad how much money is being left on the table by DIY/Indies because they aren't taking care of business.

Granted, you have heard me rake the PROs, digital aggregators, and online streamers over the coals about cheating songwriters and artists. It is obvious Kevin got cheated.

But Kevin also did not do due diligence of his own, thereby giving these entities *carte blanche* to work him over.

Royalties will be collected. But if you do not let the reporting and paying systems know you are there, whose fault is that?

What did Kevin do wrong? He signed up with a digital aggregator for publishing services allowing them to be publisher. He should only have signed up for distribution.

CURRENT MUSIC BUSINESS MODEL

Effort and Work

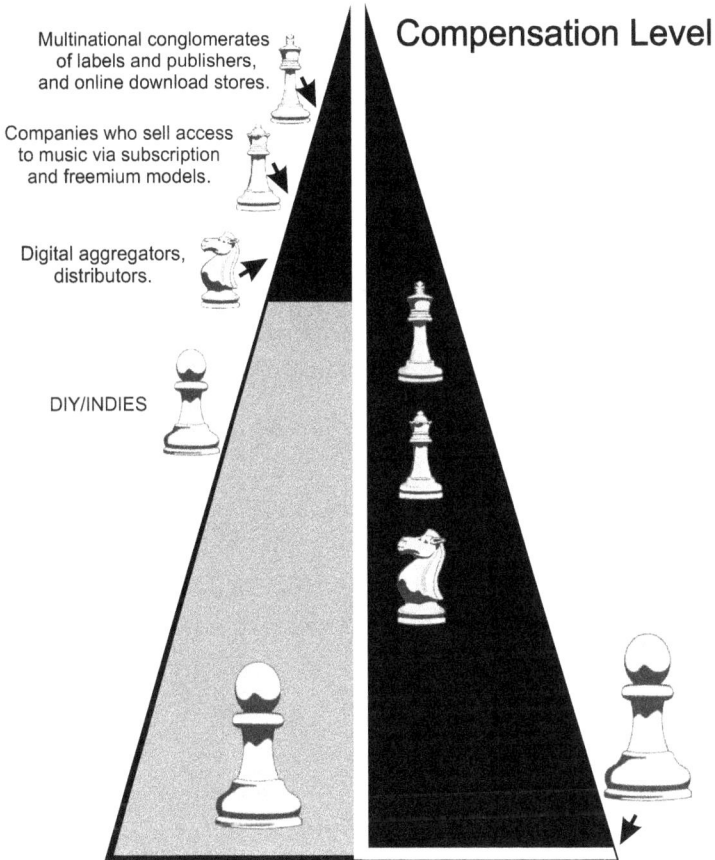

Multinational conglomerates of labels and publishers, and online download stores.

Companies who sell access to music via subscription and freemium models.

Digital aggregators, distributors.

DIY/INDIES

Compensation Level

DOES THIS SEEM UNBALANCED TO YOU?

KEEPING FINANCIAL RECORDS:

Should your DIY/Indie career grow, at some point you will need to know where you are making and losing money. A good accounting system will help. It can be as simple or robust as you need it to be.

An accountant is a person trained in keeping track of expenses and income, and generates reports showing where income is coming from, what expenses are going for and to whom, profit margins, and income statements, as well as prepping all numbers for a Certified Public Account (CPA) if need be, and the Internal Revenue Service.

Not all accountants (or CPAs) are familiar with the entertainment industry. Have accountants document their knowledge of entertainment accounting before hiring them.

CHARTING:

Unless you are a customer of Nielsen, BDS, SoundScan, or the RIAA, you will not be charting on Billboard. These companies are paid handsomely for their services by the major labels and publishers. There are plenty of charts out there on which you can place and still get the market information you need, but these are usually regional or genre-specific.

Durden's Down & Dirty Hint & Tip

Diversify your offerings to broaden opportunities to monetize your brand (merch with logo, book of lyrics) and music (vinyl, CD, tape, downloads, licensing).

CONTRACT:

An agreement between two or more parties (individuals or companies) that defines and describes actions for all parties involved, timelines for completion of actions, what will or can determine breach of contract, remedies for breach of contract, financial expectations for all parties, and duration of contractual obligations, among other things.

Good fences make good neighbors.

CONTROLLED COMPOSITION :

A song that is written, owned, or otherwise controlled by the recording artist.

CONTROLLED COMPOSITION CLAUSE:

Such a clause is language in a contract provided by a label to an artist that basically says if the person who wrote the song is also the recording artist, then the label will not pay full rate for both categories of income stream he is entitled to – artist and songwriter. (If you are going Indie all the way and are serving as your own label, this does not apply to you.)

A controlled composition clause is often presented to artists as "standard in the industry". Do not be fooled. It is often negotiable. Consult an attorney and weigh the choices carefully. Will insisting on striking the clause stop the deal in its tracks? If not, is there anything to gain by taking less money? If there isn't, why accept the clause?

Detailed conversations with attorney and label can often bring forth a document that makes winners of both parties to the deal.

ISRC:

The International Standard Recording Code (ISRC) is the international identification system for sound recordings and audio-visual recordings. Each ISRC is a unique and permanent identifier for an individual recording, independent of the format on which it appears (CD, audio, video, etc.) or the rights holders involved. Only one ISRC should be issued for a track, and an ISRC can never represent more than one unique recording. Therefore, each version of Song A will have a different ISRC.

For instance, Song A's versions could be [see next page]:

ISRCs are widely used in digital commerce by download sites. An ISRC can be permanently encoded into a product as its digital fingerprint. Encoded ISRCs provide the means to accurately identify recordings for royalty payments.

ISRC is a reliable international identification system providing a unique tool for the purpose of rights administration, as long as it is used correctly.

If you are the recording rights owner, take care to manage your own bank of ISRCs. A simple Excel spreadsheet or Word document will suffice.

ISRC coding is compatible with standards developed in the field of consumer electronics and is readable by hardware already used in the recording industry. It is cost-effective and can be put into operation without requiring a special investment in equipment or technologies. It is required by most digital distribution companies and online download sales sites.

THIS CODE USED HERE IS A SAMPLE CODE.

SONG A

VERSION	ISRC #
Clean	ISRC US-K40-14-00157
Explicit	ISRC US-K40-14-00158
a capella	ISRC US-K40-14-00159
Instrumental	ISRC US-K40-14-00160
Music Video w/Vocals	ISRC US-K40-14-00161
Music Video Instrumental	ISRC US-K40-14-00162
a capella video	ISRC US-K40-14-00163
Clean, feat.	ISRC US-K40-14-00164
Explicit, feat.	ISRC US-K40-14-00165

...and so forth, you get the picture.

ISRC SYNTAX

ISRC QM-K40-14-00212 or ISRC QM K40 14 00212

Code Identifier: ISRC
Country Code (2 characters) QM
Registrant Code (3 characters) K40
Year of Reference (2 digits) 14
Designation Code (5 digits) 00212

ISRC agencies can be found in 57 countries. To find an agency in your country in order to get proper country code visit **isrc.ifpi.org/en/**

Each individual mastered work (song) ready to be released into retail environments via downloaded tracks or physical media (vinyl, CDs, tapes), or performed on radio or through streaming services, can be tracked through ISRC and other means. Not everyone will be able to qualify for an ISRC registrant code. You must hold the rights to the recording or be a high-volume manager. If you do not fit these categories, you may need to register with an ISRC manager. Go here for more –

ifpi.org/content/library/isrc_handbook.pdf

If there is a change in the ownership of a recording, the ISRC should not be changed. Once an ISRC has been assigned, the identity of the registrant itself cannot and should not be used to directly imply ownership. This is in keeping with the principle that the ISRC is to *identify a particular version of the recording* rather than other factors such as ownership at a given point in time.

Ownership rights often change; therefore ownership data should be held in separate databases where it can be updated when necessary. The ISRC can then be used to look up information about the identified recording. The role of ISRCs is to give clarity about which recording is the subject of interest.

NOTE: An ISRC is not required if –
- You are only selling direct-to-fan via CD sales at concerts or from your website or downloads through a website such as Bandcamp.com or any service that simply facilitates a retail transaction between you and a consumer, and if —

- That payment goes straight into your PayPal or other account you've set up to receive these funds.
- You have no intention of having your music played through streaming services.
- You will not have your music played on terrestrial, non-interactive, or interactive Internet radio.
- A third-party retailer will not be involved in the sale of your inventory, whether it sells via iTunes or other retail digital or brick-and-mortar stores, or is distributed by any service where royalties are calculated and paid to you directly or through a performing rights organization, SoundExchange.com, a music library, or other royalty-tracking or payment service provider.

However, if you plan on putting music into any retail environment wherein you consign your inventory (albums, CDs, digital content) into another company's sales channel, you must have your own branded UPC and ISRC identifiers to maintain clear ownership and/or control.

**Look up ISRC on SoundExchange.com:
tinyurl.com/y8udrwy8**

Durden's Down & Dirty Hint & Tip

Don't chase the record deal. Those are everywhere! Instead, let them chase you. That puts you in a power position at the bargaining table. Don't be eager to sign.

TECHNOLOGY:

Management of processes that formerly required a large investment of time, expensive equipment, and/or hard-to-find expertise of skilled individuals is now handled through technology.

On the production side, think about software plug-ins in your favorite recording and mixing software suites used for music and video production, which organize a multi-step process into a one-click solution. Don't be a slave to technology iterations. You will go broke.

PRODUCER:

A term often misused to include anyone who makes a beat; however, making beats does not a producer make.

Producers understand how the elements of the entire song go together and help put those in place. Sometimes engineers serve as producers and producers serve as engineers. Lines can be blurred. If the producer is a collaborator in the creative process, the producer will be on the split sheet, thus entitled to a percentage of future royalties from performance and licensing.

If the producer requires payment to do the work, have a **Work-for-Hire Contract**. Producers can be in on the deal for a combination of split sheet and upfront payment, but then the percentage on the split sheet for the producer will be lower because of upfront compensation received.

Durden's Down & Dirty Hint & Tip

When it is time to scale up your market reach, that is the time to think of partnering with a label, but not before. *Remember: Have power position at negotiating table!*

VENUE REPORTING HISTORY:

If an artist wishes to remain completely DIY/Indie, keeping excellent records of where and when performances were delivered – as well as audience size, and whether tickets were sold or cover charges collected – paves the way for better business decisions and more efficient planning, and attracts investors such as officers at lending institutions who can pull the trigger on your loan.

For those looking to get signed by a label or publisher, or looking to attract other investment funding, then having historical data tracking live performances (*with a band or live instrumentation, **but not singing to a track***) allows artists to prove they are monetized, have a following, and have a disciplined work ethic.

In other words, it gives investors sound business reasons for choosing who to go into business with or lend money to.

Your venue reporting history should include:

*   Samples of advertising (flyers, posters) that include date, time, venue, band or artist name, and whether or not the band or artist is headliner, opener, or otherwise on the performance roster.
*   Video compilation of your live performances.
*   Attendee count.
*   Whether or not the event required a cover, a ticket, or was free to the public.
*   Venue name and total audience capacity.

LEAD SHEET:

It's a shocker, but sometimes sidemen don't show up for gigs and stand-ins must be hired at the last minute. Lead sheets help stand-ins get up to speed quickly on complicated or highly specific arrangements.

Professional musicians, sidemen, and singers usually know covers, so if you are a cover performer, you don't need lead sheets. **A LEAD SHEET IS A *MUST* FOR ANYBODY WHO IS *PERFORMING ORIGINAL WORKS* AND MIGHT HAVE TO RELY ON SIDEMEN.** For instance: If you are a band of one or two and need a drummer, bass player, pianist, whatever, and you hire those in each city, *you will not want to suck onstage because you asked your de facto band to guess at what you needed.*

A lead sheet is a concise written map of a song containing title, composer, lyricist, time signature, tempo, lyrics, chords and/or key, and any other information needed to perform a particular work (song). Sometimes lead sheets include the melody line for whichever instrument carries the melody.

A lead sheet is organized by verse, chorus, and bridge, and instrument. It is used by professional musicians during rehearsal and onstage during a performance of music, especially if it is music with which they are not familiar.

You should have one lead sheet per instrument required as they will each have their own expertise in their instrument and will carry different parts of the song. Lead sheets are not horribly difficult to prepare for most singer/songwriter or bands' tunes. Keep your lead sheets as PDFs on your computer (or on the cloud with a service such as Dropbox), so you can easily email to potential sidemen and singers, and/or print and bring to the show.

MECHANICAL ROYALTIES:

IF YOU ARE A DIY/INDIE who acts as his own label and publisher, and if you are NOT placing your music with other artists, you do not need to read this section. But if you are planning on pitching your songs to other artists to include on their albums or release as singles, read on:

Mechanical royalties is the term representing an agreed-upon percentage of sales of physical inventory distributed to and offered for sale at brick-and-mortar stores, whether big box or mom-and-pop, or ordered from online retailers such as Amazon.com and so forth, or sales through digital downloads.

Mechanicals, as mechanical royalties are often referred to, are per-unit payments made by the record company to the music publisher for the reproduction of copyrighted musical compositions. Labels determine the percentage a publisher or songwriter receives based on either physical units manufactured (best case), physical units shipped (acceptable case), or physical units or downloads actually sold (worst case).

There are significant financial differences among the three methods of tallying units.

When signing a mechanical royalty deal, be very careful of the language used to define the term "sold" that royalties will be based on. There is a move toward paying mechanical royalties for digital download sales. As of this writing, that is unevenly applied. It is such a mess that there is no way to comment upon it in such a way as to make it any clearer.

UPC (Universal Product Code):

The Universal Product Code is a machine-readable barcode that identifies all products (except book-related products*) to retailers. One cannot choose a UPC prefix or number. One applies for and then is assigned an overall country and company prefix from gs1us.org, then instructions are issued for the use and how to assign to product.

Small but growing music businesses working to expand their distribution channels to include large and/or national retailers that are using barcodes purchased from resellers will soon discover they need to use their own branded GS1 company prefix, and must apply other GS1 Standards to conduct business with mass retailers. Contact gs1us.org – or the agency that is authorized in your country – to license branded GS1 company prefixes.

Your business can then create unique UPC barcodes for each of your songs, albums, or branded products. Using your own UPC will protect your company's brand identity as songs or albums travel the supply chain, whether through brick-and-mortar stores or online resellers. By using additional GS1 Standards to identify product as well as share and synchronize data, DIY/Indies have better opportunity to realize operational benefits and growth.

Book-related products use ISBN for tracking. ISBN stands for International Standard Book Numbering system.

UPC ADMINISTRATOR/MANAGER:

A company or individual approved by the gs1.org agency, or its sub-agencies in each country, to properly handle the branded UPC registration paperwork for other companies or individuals.

UPC RESELLERS:

UPC resellers have their company name as the brand, not your company name. Do not be fooled: That stops your ability to sell into the retail supply chain independent of the UPC reseller.

SAMPLE UPC BARCODES: They may look different, but the same information is carried in each version. Size is chosen based on available space on the product's printed label. A white background is always required. In this sample, the UPC code has 11 digits that represent the company and the product. The last number is the check digit. It must be included.

EAN-13 BARCODE:

International version of the UPC product barcode that is fast being used across the board for products going into the retail pipeline. Nowadays mostly interchangeable with the UPC. Contrary to popular opinion, EAN-13 and UPC, and ISBN and ISBN-13 (solely for books) barcode numbers cannot be randomly generated by a user. *One must apply for a number from governing agencies.*

SAMPLE EAN-13 BARCODE: These, too, can come in varying sizes, and the same information is carried in each version. Size is chosen based on available space on the product's printed label. A white background is always required. In this sample, the EAN code has 13 digits that represent the company and the product.
The last number/symbol is the check digit. It must be included.

WORK-FOR-HIRE CONTRACT:

A contract between you and each session musician, producer, engineer, and/or session singer **not on the split sheet**. You must have a contract for each person in order to confirm clearances.

THIS IS A MUST **if you ever want your music to be included in films, TV shows, video games, advertising campaigns, or other such uses.**

NOT HAVING this contract for each non-split-sheet entity on a song WILL BE A DEAL BREAKER with those you want to license it to.

Many items in a good work-for-hire contract include, but are not limited to, spelling out the following:

- Their future royalty claims will be zero.
- They are being hired to perform, produce, or engineer bringing to bear their talents for the betterment of the work/song.
- Scope of their use of the recorded materials is defined.
- The work belongs to the person hiring (which is you), and you can sell it, perform it, and use it in any way you see fit without their permission.
- They are not allowed to sell, perform, or stream it without explicit permission from you.
- You can use their name and likeness in marketing and promotional materials – this point is completely negotiable, of course, and depends on what you will be doing with the work/song.
- They agree to perform said duties for $X.

- Names of the song or songs to be performed.
- They admit for all time they have no claim to future royalties no matter which planet or solar system the work/song is played in or which transmission method is used, whether now known or yet to be discovered.
- The date(s) of work performed.
- The location of the recording session(s).
- That payment will be given after the work is performed to your satisfaction and only via a disinterested third-party trackable method (i.e. check or money order, *but never cash because a cash transaction does not have a third-party validation built in*).
- Both parties sign and date the agreement.

These are the important components that must be included in any work-for-hire contract, but an attorney should be consulted to create contracts (including work-for-hire and other uses) that protect your individual or corporate interests, comply with state and federal laws, and are fair to those hired.

Durden's Down & Dirty Hint & Tip

Strike while the iron is hot. Don't depend on any one income stream to save the day. Be prepared to pivot with your audience and the marketplace.

LINER NOTES:

Fans want to connect with you. But until cloning gets to be mainstream, you can't be with each fan all the time. So, what can you do?

Enter liner notes. Liner notes used to be some of the best parts of album covers and inserts. Liner notes helped the fan connect with the artist or band. They generated goodwill, loyalty, and more sales of concert tickets, albums, and merch.

But with the coming of the digital age, liner notes fell into disuse. After all, on a digital album, where does the artist put the insert?

However, liner notes are making a screaming comeback. For the DIY/Indie producing their own albums, including inserts is one of the most affordable and easiest ways to let the fan "take you home" with them. Liner notes can include:

- Lyrics to songs in order presented on album;
- production team information, including musicians and background singers;
- song or project backstory;
- your motivation story;
- something personal;
- what makes you tick;
- what you like and dislike and why;
- and photos.

Make the text large enough to read easily. Also, make sure that the text weight is heavy enough to be read if it is printed over background color or a photo. Always check spelling.

GENRE:

Category that identifies a type of music. Music charting companies use genres as a way to categorize songs that chart. Lines are blurring between genres and making it more difficult to accurately place songs squarely in any one category. Some recognized genres now are:

Acid Jazz	Jazz
Alternative	Latin
Blues	Latin Pop
Bluegrass	Latin Rhythm
Broadway	Mexican
Children's	New Age
Comedy	Other
Contemporary Classics	Pop
Contemporary Jazz	R&B
Country/Americana	R&B/Hip Hop
Christian	Rap
Christian/Gospel	Reggae
Classics	Regional
Classical	Rock
Dance/Electronic	Singer/Songwriter
Folk	Traditional
Gospel	Traditional Jazz
Hard Rock	Tropical
Holidays/Seasonal	Vocal/Accoustic
Hip Hop	World

Genre blending and bending is what makes music live. Don't be afraid to do that. Art is about surprise.

RELEASE (MUSIC):

A release is a song from an artist that becomes available for sale or distribution to the general public. If a song is offered at no charge to the public, whether in physical media or by digital download, the song is now said to have been released.

Once a song is released, First-Run Rights have been given up.

If your business model includes pitching your songs for placement with other artists, do not "release" all your songs. Instead, *only* release those songs (under your artist or band name) that you do not plan on placing on other artists' albums.

HOLD BACK your best potential money-makers so that you can have profitable wiggle room when you negotiate First-Run Rights. **Protect the earning power of your catalog.**

FIRST-RUN RIGHTS:

First-run means a song is new to the listening public, has not been placed on an album, and has not been released as a single via any retail form, even as a free download for marketing/promotional purposes.

FIRST-RUN RIGHTS USUALLY COMMAND A LARGER LICENSING FEE FOR PLACEMENT WITH AN ARTIST OR IN AN AD CAMPAIGN, MOVIE, OR TV SHOW.

Covers of songs (second, third, fourth, etc. releases of a recording) most often fall under a compulsory mechanical license. These licensing fees are almost always much lower than for a first-run release.

MASTER RECORDINGS:

There can be more than one master recording of any one song. There is the first recording of it for commercial release (during which First-Run Rights can bring greater returns). The next recordings are called covers (even if the original artist or songwriter records it). Each can have its own master and each will have its own ISRC.

Whoever pays for the recording session usually owns the rights to that recording session's final version, or master.

SOUNDEXCHANGE.COM:

A performing rights organization operating under the authority of the U.S. Copyright Office. The royalties that SoundExchange.com collects and distributes are for the featured artist and the sound recording copyright owner when their work is broadcast by non-interactive digital radio. To download a list of all non-interactive Internet-based radio outlets that set playlists currently licensing from SoundExchange.com, go to this website:

soundexchange.com/about/our-work/digital-radio-providers/

Do not leave money on the table. If you have released music on any Internet-based streaming or radio company, you might have money coming to you from SoundExchange.

Durden's Down & Dirty Hint & Tip

Keep each song's ownership path clean and clear. You are the beginning to the metadata transparency in the music business.

METADATA:

Information embedded into a song containing copyright information and other data needed for tracking spins and plays, and sales within a retail environment. Incomplete, inaccurate, or non-existent metadata equals no royalties paid to you. (See SoundExchange.com's website for an example of the huge list of people they owe royalties to but cannot pay because of inaccurate or missing metadata. Might you be on this list?)

SoundExchange list: tinyurl.com/y7bt3ouf

Metadata is only part of the copyright information you must collect to prove one-stop status (see One-Stop Shop in the Be Aware section). Metadata is used for tracking in retail sales and royalty-payment systems, but is not meant to, nor can anybody claim it can, do the complete job of helping protect and defend your I.P. rights.

PROMOTER:

A person or a company that markets and promotes live events such as concerts/gigs, sports contests, professional wrestling, festivals, raves, nightclub performances, etc.

Durden's Down & Dirty Hint & Tip

Every collecting agency and organization you register your works with means they touch the money before you see it. Be selective and understand what each does for you before you allow them to represent you.

MANAGER — BUSINESS:

A person, team, or company hired by the artist to handle the day-to-day business of an artist or songwriter. Serves as liaison between artist or songwriter and others who are working for or with an artist or songwriter to confirm that projects are kept on schedule, royalties paid properly, sales booked, concert tickets sold, budgets met, and much more.

A business manager identifies potential problems and offers solutions to the artist or songwriter, and provides up-to-date reports on matters that affect business goals.

In order to need a business manager, you must have a business to manage. That is, a business that is already running and making money.

MANAGER — PERSONAL:

A person, team, or company hired by the artist or songwriter to handle personal life outside the business arena. May need to liaison with the business side.

PUBLISHER:

A publisher looks for opportunities to place songs (works) from their catalog into upcoming projects, including yet-unplaced works and those previously released (what is also known as *the back catalog*).

Publishers make deals for writers they represent. Publishers recoup out-of-U.S. royalties and collect and pay royalties to writers in licensing deals outside the scope of responsibility of the U.S. performing rights organizations.

COPYRIGHT:

As soon as an original idea (intellectual thought) leaves the mind and is fixed in a tangible form — that is, recorded in a fixed form that others can see, touch, or hear — the creator has immediately established copyright to that intellectual property, or I.P.

For instance, a live performance is not copyrighted, but a *recorded* live performance is immediately copyrighted.

These principles are the basis of the copyright laws in the United States; other countries may have differing laws regarding copyrights and intellectual property.

COPYRIGHT INFORMATION MANAGEMENT:

The process wherein content creators keep track of all phases of the creative process, including proof of creation, payment to others for services rendered (see Work-for-Hire Contracts), and split sheets between co-creators or collaborators, among other necessary data items.

Copyright Information Management (CIM) protects owners' stakes in a work so that when copyright has to be defended in a court of law or in other legal disputes, a provable chain of evidence exists to support the correct ownership.

Additionally, by having a consistent, complete record of each person's role with the work, business such as royalty and mechanical payments, as well as licensing deals, can be conducted faster and more accurately.

SPECIAL DETAILED SECTION
ON COPYRIGHTS
IN A MUSICAL WORK

COPYRIGHT 1:

The first copyright is to a song itself (melody/composition). The writer owns this copyright entirely until the writer enters into an agreement with a publisher. Then the copyright is shared between the writer and the publisher. They have a written agreement called a split sheet.

Copyright to a song ensues once it has been placed in a fixed format whether that is recorded on paper, tape, CD, and/or other format. For this basic copyright to ensue the song does not have to be retail-ready, mastered, or even released for the public to buy or stream.

Writers are often prodded to spend money registering their copyright to songs that clearly have never been recorded for retail release. This is a waste of money and time.

And why is that? Fair enough question. It is because the registered copyright is ONLY for the recorded or written version uploaded to the government at that time.

Therefore if the song changes substantially (as many songs do on their way to becoming the final version), you've just blown a huge amount of money on something that will never make it to the light of day.

FINAL recordings released for retail distribution can be (but are not legally required to be) registered with the government at Copyright.gov by the owner of the master. Just before that song is released, the writer can (but is not legally required to) register the lyrics with Copyright.gov.

IN ALL CASES that is why it is very important that this symbol (c) or this one © or the word COPYRIGHT is followed by a year and a name and be affixed to all versions of a song like this:

Where Artist, Songwriter, Publisher are same entity:
© YEAR Writer Name and Publishing Company Name

In the case of multiple writers or publishing companies:
© YEAR Writer1 Name and Publishing Company1 Name
and
© YEAR Writer2 Name and Publishing Company2 Name

YEAR means the year the song was written down for the first time whether or not it is a final version.

However, if the song is to be released for purchase (or other public performance whether that is terrestrial or Internet radio, club DJ, streaming, etc.) now you have to think about how the money flows.

It is only the publisher that has the right to license the use of that song. It is only the publisher that gets paid for the use of that song by others. That is, in a licensing situation, the money for both the writer and the publisher is paid to the publisher, who then disburses the writer's share to the writer. So you better trust who you go into business with and have signed and verified contracts for each song.

If a song is played over the airwaves, then a performing rights organization receives that money and disburses to both publisher and writer.

In any case this is money ONLY for the I.P. rights to the owners. The calculations for that fee vary based upon a myriad of factors that can change based on each individual case and contract.

But what about the retail-ready song? What about the artist? How does the artist get paid? This is where it starts to get interesting.

If the artist is the writer and publisher, then this is a more simplified process, but not by much.

Intellectual property rights have copyright that belongs to the creator, or a company or other individual who hired someone else to produce it.

But, a completely different copyright ensues for the actual final retail-ready recording. Let's say you come out with a second version of the song. Now comes...

COPYRIGHT 2 of Song version 1.

But then you put your song to a video and put it up on Vimeo or YouTube or your website or wherever. Now comes...

COPYRIGHT 3 of Music video 1.

For each version of your song and each different video you put out there, you have now established a completely different copyright. It can go on ad infinitum.

For every version of a song the artist records that is to be released to the general public, a different copyright accrues and must be claimed. That public claim will look like this:

One song, one writer, one publisher:
Wishes and Snow
© 2018 Angela K. Durden (SESAC) and Second Bight Publishing (SESAC)

One song, two writers, two publishers:
Wishes and Snow
© 2018 Angela K. Durden (SESAC), John L. Doe (ASCAP), Second Bight Publishing (SESAC), Two Bights Publishing (ASCAP)

One song, two writers, three publishers:
Wishes and Snow
© 2018 Angela K. Durden (SESAC), John L. Doe (ASCAP), Second Bight Publishing (SESAC), Two Bights Publishing (ASCAP), JLD Publishing (ASCAP)

Every writer and publisher involved will be listed. Broken down for one song as one songwriter, one publisher.

Line One: Song Title
(If versioned, then something that differentiates it from another recording of the song.)

Line Two: © YEAR Writer Name (PRO affiliation, if any) and Publishing Company Name (PRO affiliation, if any)
YEAR for writer and publisher is the year the song was first conceived. PRO means performing rights organization. In the U.S. these are: SESAC, ASCAP, BMI. If you are not in the U.S., your country

performing rights organization will be different.
Line Three: © YEAR Artist Name
© Releasing Label Name
Featured Artist (if they exist)
YEAR is the year of retail-ready release, not the year it is recorded.

But you want to know who pays the artist, right?

If the artist is acting as writer, publisher, artist, and label, bookkeeping will be very simple as all money will flow to the artist, though not in one check and not all at the same time, and sometimes it could be months or years before that money is received.

But if the artist signs with a label, the artist may only get paid for a small portion of the physical sales (including purchased downloads). These are called mechanicals. There are some industry standards though all parties to the deal can negotiate those as they please in a private agreement.

Unless otherwise agreed upon with the label, the artist probably will not get paid too much (if at all) for radio play or streaming as these rates are mandated by the government. (This is where SoundExchange should be looked into.)

That's why the label likes to "sign" artists.

If the label fronts all the money for the recording, the label will have contracts with producers and studios that will be paid before the artist is. The general flow of disbursed income goes like this:

Label pays production, marketing, distribution, and manufacturing bills first.

Label pays publisher for rights to record their version(s).

Label pays itself (always before artist).

Label pays artist (always last). [NOTE: Do not mistake label advances for money the artist can keep. Advances are loans and are always recouped against sales. If sales are low, the artist has to pay off the loan. Thus the one-hit wonder and the old "broke-ass millionaire" reference.]

Publisher receives from label, then pays writer per their split agreement.

Performing rights organizations pay publisher and writer (in some, but not all, instances).

Licensing rights for (a) Song words and (b) Song melody to be used in Situation 1, Situation 2, etc., are negotiated on a per use basis. That is, only the words are licensed, only the music is licensed, the two together can be licensed, or stems and pieces of each can be licensed.

Therefore, several contractual agreements can exist for one song. These are, or can be, between:

• Writer and publisher.
• Publisher and label.
• Label and artist (in certain instances).
• Publisher and written lyric distributor.
• Publisher and ad agency, film, TV, stage show, etc.
• Label and ad agency, film, TV.

A split sheet is the agreement between co-owners of intellectual property: Writer/composer and publisher.

Licensing rights are never listed on a split sheet because the entity asking permission to use that intellectual property is not a co-owner.

Licensing rights are granted by you for a *fee* you set and that is paid to you by a company for the use of your song for a set period of time in a set environment.

In other words, the fee will be less for one song in a local ad campaign for one month than for one song in a movie which will be played internationally then sold as a DVD with the song forever embedded in it.

It is at this time you should ask yourself what you expect of the business and take steps to protect yourself for each role you are acting in: Songwriter. Publisher. Artist. Seller of songs/albums. Licensor. Collaborator.

Improper, incomplete, or non-existent paperwork is always the undoing of a deal and kills future income streams.

There may be only one of you, but you have a stack of different hats on your head. Each can make profit or put future earnings of your I.P. in jeopardy.

COPYRIGHT REGISTRATION:

Registration of a copyright with Copyright.gov should occur only when the intellectual property is in its final form — that is, no more changes are expected — and it is getting ready to be released for sale to the general public; placed in a movie, TV show, and/or ad campaign; or getting radio or streaming play. The only version that should be registered is the final version of the work.

ATTORNEY:

A person with a **legal degree** who is **licensed** in one or more states to provide legal advice and services such as transact business, draw up contracts, and/or represent his client in a court of law. Attorneys advise clients on possible consequences to the client's business. Unless an attorney is a business partner, attorneys do not make business decisions for clients, and instead simply advise, support and, possibly, repair.

— **Entertainment Attorney:** An attorney who specializes in entertainment business deals and related matters.

— **Copyright and Intellectual Property (I.P.) Attorney:** An attorney who specializes in contracts and deals concerning the protection, sale, and licensing of intellectual property in a variety of forms, as well as the sale of copyrights.

Durden's Down & Dirty Hint & Tip

A great entertainment attorney is not an expense. **It is an investment** in your understanding of the business so that you can maximize your earning potential.

INTELLECTUAL PROPERTY (I.P.):

Intellectual property is an idea in a fixed form (recorded in some form or fashion). It can be sold, inherited, licensed to others for use, bequeathed in a will, and have its copyright registered. I.P. can be owned by an individual, a group of individuals, a business, or a corporation.

It can be created under a work-for-hire contract for a label, individual, or other entity. If an individual has been hired to create in a work-for-hire environment, the contract must be carefully read to determine what amount, if any, of that work is owned by the actual creator.

One cannot assume all or any percentage of copyright ownership accrues in work-for-hire arrangements.

FAIR USE:

Under U.S. copyright law, "fair use" allows but limits reproduction of a copyrighted work to certain purposes, such as criticism, news reporting, teaching, and research.

"Fair use" does not include small-quantity recordings made by anybody, even if for or by charities or religious organizations; nor does it exempt recordings that are distributed without charge.

Sometimes the distinction between "fair use" and infringement is not clear. Always consult an attorney if you are going to distribute any recordings you do not own the underlying copyright to.

Just because someone claims the use of a work falls under the "fair use" statute does not mean it will hold up in a court; willful copyright infringement can carry statutory damages of up to $150,000 per incident.

Do you have music that is on any non-interactive streaming service such as an Internet radio station? Are you the rights holder to any songs? Are you an artist? Are you getting as many types of royalties as possible that have been collected on your behalf from Internet activity? How do you know?

IS IT SIMPLE TO FIND LOST ROYALTIES?

YES!

But you have to take the time.

If you have not checked with SoundExchange.com, you could be missing out. To learn what they collect and for whom, and how you can see if they have any royalties for you, go to this link:

tinyurl.com/y9ca5pwq

KEN BONFIELD SAYS: Learn to live with delayed gratification. There are no weekly paychecks for DIY/Indies.

Putting the "business" in your music business.

Contributing to our difficulty in surviving the music business, we've got economic downturns, technology revolutions, and no clear path through what should by now be considered a mature and stable industry. Further, and importantly, there is a huge reluctance by many to properly complete required paperwork.

Okay. So, it's all bad news; yet here you are, still in the business. Why? Because there is opportunity. But the opportunity can only be taken advantage of if you get a map and only if you follow it. And that means:

- paperwork
- promotion
- show prep
- proper business structure
- budgeting
- merch
- those things that go into running a business and making it viable.

All must be done.

Pretending to be a diva and saying "But I'm a creative. All that is *boooooo*ring. I just want to be *a star* and have rabid fans *buying my stuff* and *talking about me* on social media all the time so I can live in a mansion somewhere expensive" does not work for long.

We still have a big problem...don't we?

At some point an artist is going to have to understand the business they are in, how it is changing, and what they must do consistently. There is no point in trying to run your music business the way the majors do — you will be taken advantage of, and sink.

Unless you establish a strong business foundation, protect and defend your intellectual property, sign documents establishing the basis for your deals, and do what it takes to build a loyal following, nobody — including friends and family — is ever going to be interested in investing in you.

Okay. So, let's say that I'm the artist, I have a following, and sales of merch and music. Now I want to take it on the road and grow a bigger fan base. What then?

This is where you now start plugging in *fee-based* label services and performance development companies.

Yes, fee-based. When you go get your oil changed, you don't say to the guy "Hey, I'll let you change my oil and then I'll use the car for a while and see if that works." Try it and the service writer will laugh you out of the lobby. You pay for a service — an oil change — and you get it.

So, let's say that you want to go on tour, but you don't have a clue how to make that happen. You hire someone that does that. They know the costs and logistics for planning and execution of a tour.

For instance, let's say you want to do a city-wide tour, or a regional or national tour. The bigger and longer the tour, the more the cost, and the more parts that must be moved around. The complication factor ramps up exponentially. It is difficult being The Act and Tour Manager at the same time. Different skill sets are required. If you are both The Act/Band (serving the audience) and the Tour Manager (serving The Act/Band), who will look after you? Burnout and health problems are not unheard of.

Are you a solo artist and all you have is your guitar? That's much easier to plan and less expensive. But are you a band? Now for each person in the band, you've just ramped up the costs for lodging, hauling instruments, load-ins/load-outs, and much more.

What about booking venues? How do you know what size venue to book? How do you know if you have a fan base to support ticket sales in certain venues in the cities you're touring? That's where charting helps you determine where to go in the first place.

How does one chart? Radio promotion comes in here. Pick a region you want to target. Get to the radio stations. Find out who they report to. Find out your place on that chart. How much play rotation are you getting? When you finally are ready to book a tour in that area, you hope that people will recognize your name.

There are a lot of moving parts and it is complicated. All doable, though. Ah, you hear a *but* coming on. *But...*

...none of this can be done scattershot.

SURVIVAL

Billy Corgin

of The Smashing Pumpkins
when interviewed
on Bloomberg Television:

"If artists cannot
self-sustain,
what is the point?
Artistic independence
is incumbent on your
ability to navigate
business successfully."

KEN BONFIELD

KenBonfield.com

Know what you do best and work it.
Never take *Maybe* for an answer.
Do not be afraid to "sell" yourself.

Q: Ken, you mentioned a big problem you have with your performing rights organization, BMI, is that they will not help you with removing someone off your publishing after the deal ran its course.

KEN: This has been a thorn in my side since 2010. I was assured it was taken care of, but when I was moving my catalog to CD Baby [for distribution only] I did some checking on my BMI member portal, and found the co-publisher was still listed. I received a check from BMI literally moments after our phone call. I was happy to get the almost $500 but chagrined to know the co-publisher received a similar amount. Money rightfully due me.

Eight years on and BMI is still sending my money to somebody else, completely ignoring the legal paperwork. I will now start the process again of phone calls, emails, and mailing of executed contracts. Thankfully I'm organized for a stoner musician. I hope I don't have to get attorneys involved as that might cost more than it's worth. I'll let you know if BMI repairs this situation.

(Editor's Note: No change with BMI situation at time of publication.)

TOP FIVE RECOMMENDATIONS
FROM KEN TO DIY/INDIES:

1. Sign up with a performing rights organization.

2. Sign up with SoundExchange.com.

3. Sign up with YouTube.com and create video content.

4. Learn to do a keyword search online. For instance, in my genre I would do a keyword search for finger style guitar, not finger picking. Then around that I would add clubs, associations, city/state/region, etc. Then get in touch. Do you know what keywords are associated with your genre or style? If not, you need to find out.

5. Find a group of like-minded peers and musicians in your region and around the country to share venues, co-bill, or even create your own festival. There is so much a good group of like-minded artists can accomplish when they work together. Search in the same way as above in number 4.

Q: Ken, you said "Most people are not aware how good they are. A vocation is an agreement with the world." What does that agreement look like?

KEN: When turning an avocation into a vocation you are saying to the world that your music is of professional quality. That it holds up against other artists in a similar genre. It says that my recordings are mastered and of the proper quality for commercial airplay.

It also means that the artist agrees to do the tasks necessary for success. For most DIY/Indie artists it means they must become their own booking agent and PR department. Also, it is very important to know how to work with sound engineers.

Each venue is different — and different every day based on the weather, even. To get your best live sound will require you and them to make tweaks to board and instrument settings, and so forth.

Know the EQ your instrument requires to sound the way you need it to, including vocal mics. I carry my own mixer and pre-amps to provide tighter control over my instrument's EQ and what I'm sending into the DI (direct input). I don't put the onus on the sound guy to make me sound good. It is his job to make the room sound good. How can I support the sound guy? See paragraph above.

The agreement about playing music for the public means the same thing it does in any profession: We do the work necessary whether we enjoy it or not so that the audience has the best experience and a memorable one.

I've taken a 16th century approach to my audience: I view them as my patrons, therefore I owe them the best sound I can produce. It is their money that allows me to live and continue to play and upgrade equipment and get the knowledge and wisdom to live a performer's life. Don't talk to the audience, talk with them, draw them in so they will continue to support you. Your performance is a conversation with the audience where *you* share feelings and stories *with them*.

This is very important: If you want to play live, learn to book yourself. I'm an active performer, well-known, and respected in my genre. I've been around for over a quarter of a century. Still, I only get asked to do about 1/3 of the shows I do now. I *still* have to actively solicit for the rest.

Do the work.

Q: Self-awareness is usually low in very talented people. How can they put on their "marketing hat" and see themselves as a fan does?

KEN: I go back to the Chet Atkins quote "If you hear something you like, and you're halfway like the public, chances are they'll like it too."

The first musical instrument I played well was the turntable. I gave myself quite an education on what great music sounded and felt like. I read liner notes as if they were the Dead Sea Scrolls. After a few years most of my friends said I had a killer taste in music. And most of it was stuff that wasn't pop or commercial. I really knew my genre, which for me is, loosely, "acoustic". But I knew the music and the players well. So, when I started composing and performing instrumental guitar music, I was pretty confident others would enjoy mine as well.

But here's the thing: You must give folks an opportunity to hear it. You're going to have to take the risk of someone not liking it. That's a risk to one's ego and self-image, but it's a necessary risk to take.

Q: Speak to the Avocation vs. Vocation mindset a bit more: What does that entail?

KEN: The life of a true artist is one of leaving the ego behind. Becoming an artist is an act of service. And *being of service* has no room for ego.

But it also means putting in the work. Playing showcases, going to industry conventions, and yes…schmoozing. U.S. business runs on who you know. It just does. You don't have to like it, but I recommend accepting it, then acting on that truth.

So, learn how to shake someone's hand confidently and look them in the eye. Put together an "elevator pitch", a short introduction describing what you do as a musician. Use the fewest words possible. Then practice it like you mean it. Have one ready for verbal encounters, and another for written communications.

If you don't get the reaction you want, ask yourself what was lacking. Then rework it. Being a professional musician is every bit as demanding as being a professional in any other job. The folks that work the hardest — and smartest — reap the most rewards. It is rarely about innate talent. The world is filled with talent, especially musical talent. Don't be quick to blame everybody else for not getting the reaction you want. Be unflinching when looking in your professional mirror.

For instance, there could be nothing wrong with your music, but *because you are targeting the wrong audience you aren't having success.* This is why it is very important to look in the mirror and be hyper-aware of the reality of the marketplace.

Find the person you know who is the most successful in your genre. Find out how they did it. Copy it if you can. And then see if you can *outwork* them. Give it a shot.

Q: Die-hard fans are still coming through for you on product and ticket sales. Are you making any new fans? If yes, how? If not, what seems to be the barrier? And what are you doing to try to build that new audience?

KEN: I've created an online persona whom I think of as Zen Ken and worked that to the hilt. I'm part of several Facebook interest groups around music and regularly post videos and guitar/music-related posts there.

I belong to several special interest forums and have grabbed fans from there. Twitter is my least effective app on social media.

I also perform at lots of luthier meetings and festivals. They are great since they attract people from all over the globe. I get to play for an international audience and those have helped me expand my fan base the most the past 5-10 years. I'm going to move into Instagram. I'll let you know how that goes.

Q: How long have you been with SoundExchange.com? What has been your experience with them? How has it affected your bottom line?

KEN: I've been with SoundExchange.com from its inception in 2003. Although I didn't know it. John Simson, who started the PRO, was my first music lawyer and contacted me when my royalties started to pile up.

It is currently my largest income stream since I've been recovering from tendinitis and unable to perform. It's been enough for me to live on as long as I am frugal. I've seen steady growth in that income, nearly doubling it since 2014.

And yes, I get both artist and label royalties.

Given that the future of recorded music appears to be in the hands of the Pandoras, Spotifys, Rhapsodys, and so forth, *all* artists who create commercial CDs and audio should register with SoundExchange.com. The composer royalties through BMI, ASCAP, and SESAC pale next to the artist/label royalties through SoundExchange.com.

Q: So, to be clear, you are with BMI and receive royalties from them, but these are significantly lower than SoundExchange.com?

KEN: Yes. The composer royalties through BMI, ASCAP, and SESAC are significantly lower compared to the artist/label royalties through SoundExchange.com.

Q: Describe a "shit gig" and why it is called that. You also called that gig a "residency". Explain that term for those who might not understand it.

KEN: One man's ceiling is another man's floor. To me a shit is a gig where the music is in the background. I haven't done a cover gig in nearly 20 years, but I've done a few shit gigs where I play in the background. These are the gigs where I insist I make a decent amount of money; $300-$1,000 depending on how deep the pockets are. I *hate* these kinds of shows as I have almost no hope of connecting with or reaching someone on a purely emotional level. These are paid practice gigs.

A residency in the music business is a regular local gig. It could be hosting an open mic, or just playing the same room every Thursday, or whatever. A residency is not necessarily a shit gig.

Over the years I've used Pat Donahue's saying about gigs. There's only three reasons to take a gig:
1) Lots of money.
2) Lots of exposure.
3) Lots of fun.

If it doesn't meet one of those requirements I don't take it. And I don't play many *exposure* gigs at this point. But I used to do that — a lot.

Q: How long have you been touring? How many live shows do you do in a year?

KEN: I transitioned into the music business, but for 25 years this has been my sole profession. I've performed well over 2000 concerts in that time. And in my peak touring years I played 150+ shows and spent 180-200 days on the road in a year. At this point in my career, and after I fully recover from tendinitis, I will play 25-30 concerts a year.

I grew up in the height of the record label system. And that was a wonderful time. I was for a time lucky to have a label behind me. And for many of us in my generation being on a record label had a huge cachet.

We want to be The Artist. We want somebody else to do the promotion and we want roadies. But that business model was only a short period of time in the history of music performance. And if that's available to you, great. Go for it. But for most of us the major label, or even independent label route isn't available.

I had to adapt to the new business model. So, I couldn't just do the booking and promotion in a half-assed way. I had to do these things well. I approach my booking as if I were my booking agent; I say and do the things a good booking agent does. When I'm doing PR, I do and say what a good PR person does. It's not the time to play the humble artist.

In my teaching, I had to learn to do lessons online via Skype. So being aware of changes and moving with those changes as quickly as time and money allows is what your DIY/Indie business will be.

Even signing with a label these days will not mitigate your responsibility toward your career.

Everybody is adapting, including Grammy winners and Knights of the British Order. Even James Taylor is building his own email list and Sir Paul McCartney and Taylor have released their own albums. So, you can do it, too.

Q: How has touring changed?

KEN: Touring has changed most in that there are very few of the Tuesday-Thursday gigs that made staying on the road a bit more doable. But house concerts have helped fill in some of those. But the biggest difference is in CD sales.

I used to be able to play for 20 people and sell as many as 30 CDs. I'd make more from sales than from the door. These days I play for 50-60 people, sometimes more, but rarely sell more than 10-15 CDs. That's a lot better than some of my peers, but it's different.

The good thing is that performance income has stayed about the same. The bad thing is that performance income has stayed about the same. I had hoped that doubling my audience would increase my income.

Sadly, that hasn't been true.

Q: What are the challenges to touring now?

KEN: For me it's the travel. I play solo, finger-style guitar music that is almost entirely original. More often than not that means hundreds of miles between gigs.

And, of course, the booking. But I just do my best to get in my "headhunter" mindset and start "dialing for dollars".

As it relates to booking: Never ask a booker for a show without offering a date for the show first. And cold calling or cold emailing isn't very fruitful. I've found that the best approach is to know about the venue. Like, who's played at that venue that is similar to you and what days of the week does your genre usually get booked. Bookers love it when you know about their venue. They respect it when you've taken the time to find out about them. And be professional on the phone if you call. Given my work is all instrumental I try to use the phone call to show my personality.

Get them to laugh. Do something to endear them to me. Make them remember who I am.

Q: We talked about how you exploit your back catalog. Can you talk about what that looks like? Can you speak on the importance of metadata management to your ability to monetize that back catalog?

KEN: Exploiting my back catalog currently meant moving my catalog from Nimbit to CD Baby. I must have missed an email along the line, but Nimbit stopped servicing the digital markets such as Spotify. I moved 4 titles to CD Baby in Dec/Jan 2018. Within 60 days, I totally recouped all the digital distributor's submission fees from the sales/royalties. It's been profit ever since. I had been paying over $200 a year for Nimbit. So, the one-time service fee for distribution services only through CD Baby is a really nice change in the bottom line. I'm expecting doubling my online income from this change within the next few months.

Another way I'm exploiting my back catalog is this: I bought 16-gig flash drives that were in the shape of a guitar. On each, I loaded 5 albums recorded at CD quality (44.1, 16 bit), plus stand-alone bonus tracks, plus PDF documents that contained tablature to 19 of my most requested songs. I then sold those at shows and workshops for a handsome profit.

Now, this was not the first time I tried to do this marketing/sales approach. I'd first tried the idea with "standard" thumb drives in 2009. The idea was cool; folks even said that at the merchandise tables after shows. But they didn't sell. At all. So I had to figure out why they weren't selling. I looked long and hard at why my first attempt failed. Then I found what would work.

Next on the agenda may be a series of "Best of" compilations. I'm considering doing something under Artistry of the Guitar and including some friends. This is still very much in the *thinking about* stage. But Will Ackerman — the man who started Windham Hill out of the trunk of his car and turned it into the Columbia Records of my genre — is a friend of mine. Ackerman sold Windham Hill Records to BMG. I've watched BMG continue to monetize Windham Hill's back catalog for almost 20 years.

If you have 3 or more albums, I think it's worth looking at your back catalog for ways to easily monetize the tracks yet again.

Q: You talked about forming alliances with industry groups, organizations, other players. Can you tell us who you've formed alliances with and how to choose that which works best?

KEN: The best thing I ever did was start "Artistry of the Guitar". It started out as a traveling festival with Peter Janson, Steve Davison, and a local instrumental guitarist from wherever we happened to be having a show. I did this from 2004 until 2013. I produced a couple of hundred in-the-round concerts with other guitarists all over North America. I got to know dozens of other guitarists. They've helped me get gigs, sell CDs, book tours, as well as inspired and educated me.

I think the Folk Alliance and other organizations are great. But what's even more powerful is when like-minded musicians get together of their own volition.

When we stop looking at our peers solely as competitors and begin seeing them as possible partners, a wider world opens and can put a career into overdrive.

Q: You mentioned that Spotify lets you see who is listening to your music. How do you make use of that to encourage fan engagement? And how do you point those listeners to your website in order to make sales or accomplish another goal?

KEN: Still learning that aspect. But it seems like it could be a way to find more fans and sell more product. I'm in the process of creating several playlists. Some of just me; for example creating a playlist of all up-tempo pieces, or all Celtic-inspired pieces I've composed, or a New Age sampler.

I've already created an "Artistry of the Guitar" playlist that has me plus a bunch of music from folks who've been part of my Artistry of the Guitar series, and I'm looking at creating a playlist purely of guitarists I enjoy and who have inspired me.

I already know my demographics; what I've learned from Spotify has just reinforced that. But what I'm learning from the playlists my music is included on is which songs folks are drawn to from my catalog. This may influence future set lists in performances, and may even influence what type of music I include in future recordings. Do more of what more people enjoy.

Q: You mentioned that there came a time when somebody told you that you did not fit in the bar-playing scene and you then went solely to ticketed events. You then commented "You have to know where you fit in and work that. Care where you play!" Can you expand on that thought process? How do you find where you fit in if you do original material?

KEN: I was actually the one that noticed where I belonged. It's not brain surgery. Ask yourself, "When was the time, venue, event, concert your music worked best?" That's what you should try to replicate.

Who does what you do? Where do they play? Does it work? If yes, play there. If not…don't.

Original music most often works in concert series, or venues in the folk world like Eddie's Attic in Decatur, Georgia; The Red Clay Theater in Duluth, Georgia (Eddie Owen's second location); The Bluebird Café in Nashville; or The Grey Eagle, Club Passim, etc. I know the acoustic world, but each artist should get to know their genre.

Who are the movers and shakers? What are the holy grail venues in your genre? What are the venues on the way to the holy grail?

Some Internet sites have tour listings, and band sites often have their tour schedules. Find folks who do what you do, see where they have played or are going to play, then hit up the venues. One tip: Make sure whatever artist you mention to the venue was well received before you try to go in on their coattails. Ask me how I know. *Exactly.*

In any case, this is the nitty gritty of touring: Research. And it's necessary. It's much easier in 2018 than it used to be even ten or twenty years ago.

I'm going to repeat myself here: Do the work.

Q: You used to be with labels but when they dropped tour support, you dropped them and formed your own independent label. Explain that.

KEN: I wish. What happened was that I was on a label, doing great, charting with two albums, and **they shut down.** I looked for — and found — other labels interested in me, but none of them offered tour support. That's when I started my own label.

When I was getting tour support and the label was behind my albums, it made sense to be on a label. And it was the mid-'90s when CDs were selling like hotcakes. Once the Internet became a real thing, and once tour support stopped being a real thing, starting my own label was a no-brainer.

Given the tools different aggregators provide musicians, there's really no need to sign with a record label these days. Signing often means giving up artistic and financial control of your effort. I believe artists can make more money off their music when they remain independent. But, it does mean you'll have to do for yourself what the label did. That, or hire folks who can do it better than you can. But you've got to do the work.

In other words, it is better to have a larger slice of a small pie than to get a sliver of a huge pie.

Q: What is your backstory?

KEN: I was an insurance headhunter from 1981-1993. I had a client pay me 120 days too late and it put me out of business. A friend heard of my predicament, knew I played guitar, and offered me a chance to play in her restaurant for lunches and dinners as often as I wanted.

That was in Taos, New Mexico, and Dory's was the name of the restaurant.

I played there almost every day, sometimes twice a day, for months. At first, I was playing all covers, and then some folks asked about originals, so I started playing originals. The tip jar kept getting filled better when I played originals, so I kept doing that.

Then Arlo Guthrie came in looking for the hot guitarist he heard about, but sadly I was being accosted by my ex-wife at the time and missed it. I would go on to play with Arlo at the Kent State Folk Festival in 1998.

A couple of weeks after Arlo, Michael Martin Murphy started to come by while I played, and we struck up a bit of a friendship. He was sitting in with me one day and during a break asked, "Where are you going to take this? You can't stay here."

We sat down with a map and started looking and he recommended Asheville, North Carolina. That was April of '94. I was in Asheville by my birthday in June that year. And the rest, as they say, is history.

Q: Fear of "No" often rules decision-making processes. What do you have to say about that?

KEN: I said this on a musician's thread on FB a week or so ago: "You know you're becoming a real artist when you say no almost as often as you say yes. It means that you know where you belong and when what you do is going to work, and when it doesn't."

Over the years I've learned to push back. I am firm in my beliefs about what works for me and what doesn't, and I won't take a gig when I know it won't work. The money gained is never enough to offset whatever concessions I've made to the venue or presenter. There are some things not worth negotiating over. Once you know what works for you, don't give in.

And as it relates to booking, I push for No's. I *hate* Maybes. I can't do anything with a Maybe because it keeps me treading water. If someone says Maybe, I ask how that gets changed to a Yes or No. I insist on specifics. And then, if I still want the gig, I do what's needed. But don't be afraid of No's; be afraid of Maybes.

Q: What did I not think to ask yet?

KEN: You've covered so much. But I will end with this. When one enters the DIY/Indie world, the onus is on you. Period. The music business is the way it is. Until the paradigm shifts again. Period. And the paradigm shift will most likely not benefit the musician. GET OVER IT. Deal with what's real.

Learn what needs to be done.

Do it to the best of your ability with no excuses and no apologies. Just do it.

In the 21st century, success will go to the same kinds of musicians it did in the 18th and 19th centuries: The ones who worked the systems they were born into. Worked them to the best of their abilities. The truth is simple: Success in music has always been about who worked the hardest, who promoted the hardest, and not who was the most talented.

Again, *do the work.*

Last thought: Learn what it is that you do best and do *that*. Don't worry about what you can't do, or what others think you should do. Do what you do best. That's who you are as an artist, and that's all you'll ever need to be.

KEN BONFIELD SAYS:

Gaming the streaming system of reporting by buying spins or hiring a company to get fake stream count only hurts you when you are no longer allowed to put your music into the stream.

I ONLY WANT ORGANIC PLAYS BECAUSE I KNOW THOSE ARE REAL.

Playlist plugging companies can be legit or not. One company is selling stream counts (50k for $150) by **using click farms and illegal hacking.** You may remember two of The Bigs did the same thing to YouTube a few years back and had to pay back millions in stolen royalties. Digital distributors are now pulling music from distribution for any artist or label using those services — which means coming off streaming services and other portals — and **withholding royalties until it is sorted out if illegal means were used.**

DURDEN SAYS

You've got to:

Make the plan.
Work the plan.
Remain flexible.
Stay proactive.
And get help.

SURVIVAL

Making money
is not **evil**
and does not
detract from
the purity of
your **art.**

Marketing dollars
are not expenses.
They are
investments in
future earnings.

BE AWARE.

You may interact with these things
at some point, so plan how to deal
with them when they come up.

ISRC MANAGERS:

The U.S. ISRC Agency has allocated registrant codes for ISRC Managers, which they can use to assign ISRCs on behalf of clients or customers, including clients who cannot qualify for their own ISRC.

ISRC Managers can provide individual ISRCs to independent artists or to those who do not wish to manage their own ISRC assignment. ISRCs are issued as a part of the business arrangement between the ISRC management company and an artist or other client, and they are assigned to only those tracks that fall within this agreement.

ISRC Managers must register with an agency authorized in their country to manage the process in order to obtain the Registrant Code necessary to assign ISRCs for recordings they do not own. ISRC Managers must agree to comply with terms set forth by the agency in order to be properly registered with it. A list of ISRC Managers is available at:

isrc.ifpi.org/en/get-isrc/isrc-managers

If you have any questions about whether a company or individual claiming to be an ISRC Manager is legitimately registered, contact the agency in your country of residence. The ISRC organization will help you understand how to construct and embed the code as part of the metadata so that you can do all in your power to accurately identify where payments should go.

HARRY FOX AGENCY (HFA):

SESAC purchased the Harry Fox Agency late in 2015. In a quick turnaround sale in 2017, SESAC owner Rizvi Traverse sold the PRO to The Blackstone Group.

HFA provides rights management, licensing, and royalty-collection services for the U.S. music industry's publishers. It acts as an agency to license, collect, and distribute royalties on behalf of copyright owners.

HFA issues mechanical licenses for products manufactured and distributed in the U.S. A mechanical license grants the rights to reproduce and distribute original copyrighted musical compositions (songs) for use on CDs, records, tapes, ringtones, permanent digital downloads, interactive streams and other digital formats supporting various business models, including cloud-based music services and bundled music services.

Because of incorrect metadata, HFA cannot pay a lot of royalties since it cannot find some of its own customers. Consistently correcting metadata information about your song is key to collecting money due you.

DIY/Indies will find huge hurdles to getting their music listed with HFA. HFA requires complete ownership proofs for each song listed with them. They only pay publishers. They do not pay artists, writers, producers, or anyone else on the split sheet.

EXECUTIVE PRODUCER:

Often provides funding for a project, and usually chooses members of and oversees an entire team to put together a song or project that can include many songs or performances. Executive producers:

- set production schedule;
- set final song(s) for project;
- choose production facility;
- choose musicians and background singers;
- set and meet marketing timelines;
- confirm all contracts are correct and in place;
- confirm payments are properly executed;
- confirm clearances for future licensing are in place;
- provide funding;
- keep track of all the moving pieces that must be in place to bring a song or project to a successful conclusion;
- confirm project is properly monetized;
- can serve as general manager;
- confirm distribution outlets;
- may also be a member of the band.

PROS: Time saving, money saving, no duplication of effort, projects come to market faster.

CONS: Can put a project into limbo. *Vet your choice closely.*

RADIO:

Radio is not in the business of helping artists. Radio is in the business of selling advertising by promising to attract ears of buyers. It chooses music to attract and keep listeners and gets music mostly from The Bigs. DIY/Indies are considered the red-headed stepchild. The kiss of death for the DIY/Indie is the "Local Hour" on a radio station.

As one promoter once put it about radio, "It's not about who is let in, it's about who can be kept out." They will keep out anyone who cannot attract ears, or those who would make them fill out extra paperwork.

RIAA:

The Recording Industry Association of America tracks sales of recordings (specifically shipments minus potential returns) on a long-term basis through its certification system. The only members of the RIAA are The Bigs, The Majors, and their wholly owned subsidiaries, as well as the distribution entities for hundreds of labels the majors control; these do not like real independents and attempt to keep them out of the mainstream outlets.

LABEL:

A company that puts together music projects with artists, might front the money for recording and/or marketing, can arrange tours, often coordinates distribution of physical product to retail outlets, sells product, collects and distributes money due the label and artist, and most often wants to own the master recordings.

A DIY/Indie most often serves as their own label.

MUSIC LIBRARIES:

As the name implies, a music library has many songs, just as the public library has many books. Music library companies assure licensees (those who want to use songs for a fee) that all the music represented for licensing has one-stop status. In other words, all clearances for a song are in place and a music library can sign off on its placement in a movie, ad campaign, TV show, etc. and the licensee is assured they have solid ground for defending a lawsuit in case they are sued.

A fee is paid to the music library, which pays the clients (usually publishers, though not always). The publisher pays other co-owners agreed-upon shares.

Music libraries often retitle. Retitling is often used as a way to separate a work and earned fees from the rightful owner.

COVERS:

A cover is any original song that has been licensed to be recorded a second time, or more. There are some songs that have been "covered" thousands of times. Not a bad income stream for the publisher(s) and writer(s) who have kept complete and proper ownership paperwork.

Durden's Down & Dirty Hint & Tip

The open dirty secret is that even if an Indie label that only has distribution through a major is selling hot and heavy, it is the major which counts those sales as their market share, never publicly mentioning the Indie labels' contributions.

PUBLISHING DEAL:

Time-limited representation agreements with publishers and labels should be read carefully and an entertainment attorney's advice sought. In no case should the contract run more than three years, nor should there be an automatic extension. Don't sign away rights to absolutely everything you create during the contract period.

Read the contract carefully. Have it reviewed by an *entertainment attorney*; you must thoroughly understand what you are signing *before* you sign it. Once a deal is signed, you are stuck with the consequences.

MEDIABASE:

Mediabase electronically monitors more than 1700 radio stations in the top 180 U.S. and Canadian markets, 24 hours a day, seven days a week. Those radio stations are broken out into specific radio "panels" and included in the most appropriate "format". It is the leading radio-monitoring service used by broadcast companies in the U.S. , and also serves almost every major recording and publishing company.

Mediabase publishes music charts and other data based on the most-played songs on terrestrial and satellite radio, providing in-depth analytical tools for radio and record industry professionals.

Mediabase charts and airplay data are used by many popular radio countdown shows and televised music awards programs. Music charts are published in both domestic and international trade publications and newspapers worldwide. Mediabase is a division of iHeart Media Inc., once known as Clear Channel Media.

U.S. formats monitored by Mediabase:

Mainstream Adult Contemporary
Hot Adult Contemporary
Mainstream Top 40
Rhythmic Top 40
Urban
Urban Adult Contemporary
Country
Alternative Rock
Active Rock
Mainstream Rock
Adult Alternative
Rhythmic Adult Contemporary
Adult Hits
Dance
Classic Rock
Smooth Jazz
Christian
Classic Hits
Gospel
Regional Mexican
Spanish Contemporary
Tropical
Christmas (Seasonal)

Canadian Radio

Top 40
Hot Adult Contemporary
Adult Contemporary
Country
Active Rock
Alternative

Mediabase charts are the source for radio countdown programs such as:

American Top 40 with Ryan Seacrest
(Top 40 and Hot AC shows)

Bob Kingsley's Country Top 40

Country Countdown USA with Lon Helton

American Country Countdown with Kix Brooks (from 2009-2017)

Crook & Chase Country Countdown

Nikki Sixx Active Rock and Alternative Radio Countdowns

SiriusXM Hits 1 Weekend Countdown

Smooth Jazz Top 20 Countdown with Allen Kepler

TUNESAT:

An independent monitoring service that uses a unique audio-recognition technology to monitor hundreds of TV channels and millions of websites around the world, helping rights holders collect millions of dollars that otherwise would have been lost.

A very large percentage of music used on television goes unreported to performance rights organizations (PROs) due to the manual reporting process, making monetizing music performances with accuracy nearly impossible.

Created by composers, this service addresses non-compliance issues to help rights holders get paid what they are due. This service could come in handy if you believe your music is being used without a licensing contract in place, and to keep music libraries honest.

TuneSat provides transparent music performance data to all its subscribers, who can then use the accurate data to recover lost royalties, and protect and defend their copyrights. The service is for anyone who wants to track their music or audio content on TV and/or the Internet, for any reason. If you believe you are not being compensated properly for these uses of your music, you may want to use **TuneSat.com** to get a handle on what is happening with your intellectual property.

The monthly fee is reasonably priced for the DIY/Indie who has music out in the world and earning. While each performing rights organization has different processes for claiming unpaid royalties, TuneSat provides the data *you* need to submit *your* claims to your PRO and work with them more efficiently to get paid what *you're* rightfully due.

ALLMUSIC.COM:

An online service that enables searching by song, album, or artist for information about released music. AllMusic.com gets its information from its data provider, TiVo Corporation. For current submission requirements see:

allmusic.com/product-submissions

TiVo provides subscribers with reviews, album liner notes, biographies, and tagged metadata like genre, style, mood, theme, and similar artists, as well as information about credits, album covers, sound clips, music videos, and more. Providing your product to TiVo is the best way to get your information listed on AllMusic.com.

There is no guarantee that your music or information will be added to TiVo's database or show up on AllMusic.com. They add products and other materials at their discretion.

A&R (Artists & Repertoire):

A person who scouts for songwriters or recording artists, matching them with labels and large publishers. A&Rs may oversee artistic development of their discoveries. Can be an employee of a label or publisher, or an independent recommending acts to a variety of labels and publishers.

A&Rs do not work for you, and are only motivated by what they believe the label or publisher is interested in. A&Rs are in sales: They are selling their professional opinion about acts that may earn a label or publisher money over time.

Not having an A&R pitch you to a label or publisher does not mean your music sucks. It does mean you don't fit their clients at this time.

CISAC (International Confederation of Societies of Authors and Composers):

A worldwide network of authors and composers' rights societies, comprising 230 collective management organizations (such as ASCAP and BMI in the U.S.) in 120 countries and tasked with protecting the interests of over 3 million creators and rights holders, promoting intellectual property rights of creators, and advancing the highest business standards to protect those rights. CISAC licenses music performing rights societies to issue the International Standard Work Code (ISWC), numbers assigned to songs by and for PROs.

BROADCAST DATA SYSTEMS (BDS):

Nielsen Broadcast Data Systems, better known as BDS, tracks monitored radio, television, and Internet airplay. If a song is detected, BDS counts the number of spins — i.e. times the song is played. To submit your released music that is being played on radio, television, or Internet, go to:

tinyurl.com/zfnq3n9

SOUNDSCAN:

Nielsen SoundScan collects information via a sales-tracking system of music and music video products throughout the United States and Canada, monitoring music consumer behavior and reporting to subscribers what music is being bought both in-store and digitally. The key to this service is accurate metadata, including ISRC and UPC codes, as well as having trackable sales.

ISWC:

The International Standard Musical Work Code (ISWC) is a unique, permanent, and internationally recognized reference number for the identification of a musical work. It is part of the CIS (Common Information System) initiative that cisac.org, the worldwide confederation of societies of authors, developed to respond to the need for information in the digital age.

ISWC is a worldwide standard approved by the International Organization for Standardization, or ISO. An ISWC begins with the letter T, followed by a nine-digit unique number with an additional check digit at the end. (Written format looks like this: T-345246800-1).

ISWCs are allocated by a qualified numbering agency only when all the creators have been uniquely identified. Thus the need for DIY/Indies to have correct, thorough, and completed paperwork as outlined in other places in this manual. Descriptive metadata that must be collected, reported, and tracked for an ISWC includes:

> Title of the work; all composers, authors and arrangers of the work identified by their IPI numbers (Interested Party Information) and role codes; the work classification code from cisac.org's Common Information System standards list; in the case of "versions," the identity of the work from which the version was made.

The ISWC uniquely and accurately identifies each specific musical work. The current identification methods of musical works, such as by work title, may at times result in confusion, especially when multiple musical works share the same or similar titles.

Since the ISWC remains permanently with a musical work, it will identify that musical work even after the work is distributed across national boundaries and in many languages.

The ISWC supports a wide range of computerized applications, particularly those involving tracking and exchange of musical works information (e.g. registration, identification, royalty distribution, and more).

The ISWC identifies musical works, not their appearance, display, object, or expression (e.g. publications, broadcasts, etc.). It does not identify recordings, sheet music, or any other type of performance associated with the musical work. The ISWC does not indicate split sheet shares of composers or copyright owners of the work, as there are often too many and they change over time.

Performing rights organizations (PROs) and other authorized agencies assign an ISWC when a work is registered with them. Owners have no control over that assignment, but can easily find out the number by looking at a song's information as it is registered with their PRO.

PERFORMING RIGHTS ORGANIZATION (P.R.O. or PRO):

An association or corporation that licenses the public performance of non-dramatic musical works on behalf of the copyright owner, and collects royalties for that license. PROs can be nonprofit, as in the case of ASCAP and BMI, or can be a privately held for-profit company, as in the case of SESAC. Over 70 countries in the world have performing rights organizations or societies.

Italy recognized a performing rights society in 1882, Germany in 1915. In the United States, The American Society of Composers, Authors and Publishers (ASCAP) was founded in 1914, followed by Broadcast Music Inc. (BMI) in 1939. They operate as not-for-profit companies whose annual reports can be found online, though these may not answer all your questions. The Society of European Stage Authors & Composers (SESAC), founded in 1930, is a privately owned company and chooses not to publicly disclose an annual report, as is its legal right.

Performing rights organizations only collect the data necessary to track spins or plays. They do not collect any other information that your business must have to prove ownership or that clears works for licensing.

BONUS:

A signing bonus is a financial payment presented to an artist or a band upon agreeing to a deal with a label or publisher. *A signing bonus does not have to be paid back.* A bonus is money you can spend immediately if you want to.

Do not confuse a bonus with an advance. The first is for keeps; the latter must be paid back.

Durden's Down & Dirty Hint & Tip

DIY/Indies live up to their name. There is a reason they are independently doing it themselves: They are looking for a better way — or a better life. DIY/Indies' search is what is driving the new music business economy. It's messy now, but there is a lot of opportunity for you.

MUSIC SUPERVISOR:

A music supervisor can be an employee of a network such as Turner Broadcasting or a film production company such as Warner Bros. They can also be employed on a work-for-hire basis by anyone who must identify the best music for use in a project such as a television show or film.

They confirm each song has one-stop licensing status (best case), or confirm all parties to the licensing of it have signed off correctly (acceptable case).

A music supervisor's main job is to confirm that the licensee will not be sued for copyright infringement, thus holding up or stopping the release of the project and wasting everybody's time and money.

ONE-STOP SHOP or ONE-STOP STATUS:

One-stop implies all clearances for a song or work can be had from a single person or entity. That is, one person or entity can sign off on a song's use in any licensing situation. Sign-off implies the licensee can rest assured it will not be sued for copyright infringement.

This status requires diligent copyright information management work flow on the part of the rights owners. **The responsibility for confirming this rests squarely on the shoulders of the creator, usually the songwriter.**

SURVIVAL

There is no one path
to what works best
in the business.
What works for one,
supports their goals,
fits into their life,
may not necessarily
work, support,
or fit another.
Don't be afraid to
tweak, change, and
reinvent the business
to suit your needs.

LICENSING

The following
section deals with
all licensing types
and other
information about
this subject you
will need to
understand before
you license a work.

AREA OF DOMINANT INFLUENCE:

The geographic area or market reached by a radio or television station. The information is used by advertisers and ratings companies to determine the potential audience of a station. Not all music plays equally on all stations.

BLANKET LICENSE:

By paying an annual fee, commercial users of music are allowed unlimited plays in a public setting of any or all songs in the repertories of performing rights organizations (PROs) such as SESAC, BMI, and ASCAP.

Blanket licenses save commercial users of music the hassles, trouble, and expense of paperwork involved in finding and negotiating licenses with all of the copyright owners of works that might be used during the licensing period. They also help prevent a licensee from infringing on the copyrights of the PROs' members and affiliates, and cover foreign writers whose music is licensed by the PROs in the U.S.

You are allowed to issue your *own blanket license* to any venue of all works *you own and control outright*. The venue will pay you. You must give a copy of the blanket license to the venue, keep one for your records, and advise your PRO of this business arrangement with the venue. Once advised of the business arrangement, no PRO can fine or sue the venue.

However, for you to get payment from a venue from issuance of your blanket license, if your music is listed with a PRO, you cannot claim any royalties from the PRO for that music. In other words, you cannot double dip.

DRAMATIC OR GRAND RIGHTS, or DRAMATIC PERFORMANCE:

Dramatic and grand rights are licensed by the composer or the publisher of the work (song). Dramatic performances involve using the work (song) to tell a story, or as any part of a storyline.

MASTER:

A master is an original final recording by an artist or band of any song. There can be many masters of the same song because many artists or bands may choose to cover a previously released song.

MECHANICAL RIGHTS:

A mechanical right is the right to record and distribute without visual images a song on a phonorecord for private use by an end user. Mechanical rights or a mechanical license must be obtained in order to lawfully make and distribute vinyl records, CDs, or tapes of songs whose copyrights belong to someone else. Licenses for recording rights controlled by some music publishers can be obtained from the Harry Fox Agency by going to its website at HarryFox.com.

These royalty rates can be negotiated individually by the copyright holders. First-Run Rights can significantly increase mechanical royalties.

MECHANICAL RIGHTS, COMPULSORY:

Same as Mechanical Rights except they are for a composition that has already been commercially recorded and released to the general public. If someone wishes to record and distribute that composition and they are not the original songwriter, they must obtain a compulsory mechanical license from the current copyright owner. The requirements of the compulsory mechanical license are outlined in Section 115 of the U.S. Copyright Act of 1976.

To be entitled to receive royalties under a compulsory mechanical license, the copyright owner must be identified in the registration or other public records of the Copyright Office.

For each work (song) embodied in the phonorecord, the royalty rate is set by law. Depending on the length of the song and the year it was released, royalty rates fluctuate. As of this writing, the rate has not risen above a dime per copy.

The royalty rate for a compulsory mechanical license can be negotiated in a private deal between the copyright owner and the licensee who wants to cover and/or distribute the song. If the paperwork is complete and signed by all parties, privately negotiated rates directly between the copyright owner and the licensee do not break the law of compulsory mechanical licensing.

PER PROGRAM:

A per-program license is similar to a blanket license in that it authorizes a radio or television broadcaster to use all the works in a performing rights organization's repertoire. The license is designed to cover use of PRO members' music in a particular radio or television program, and compels the user to keep track of all music used. If the user wishes to place music in programs not covered by the license, the user must obtain the proper licensing rights.

PRINT:
Sheet music with lyrics. Sheet music without lyrics. Printed lyrics without music notation. This can include lyrics used in a book, written on a chalkboard in a movie scene, or seen anywhere the printed word can be read and distributed for a profit.

PUBLIC PERFORMANCE or PERFORMANCE RIGHTS:
Music that is played in a place open to the public, or where the significant number of persons assembled is larger than the friends-and-family circle. A public performance can also occur when the performance is transmitted by means of any device or process (for example, via broadcast, telephone wire, or other means) for the public to hear. In order to perform a copyrighted work publicly, the user must obtain performance rights from the copyright owner or his representative.

RECORD LABEL:
A record label or company makes, distributes, and markets sound recordings (CDs, tapes, vinyl, and so forth). Record labels obtain from music publishers the right to record and distribute covers of songs by paying licensing fees.

RETRANSMISSION:

A **transmission** of a performance is sent by any device or process (examples: Radio, TV, cable, satellite, telephone) and received somewhere else.

A *retransmission* is an additional transmission of that performance from radio, etc. to yet another place.

SOUND RECORDING:

A sound recording refers to the copyright of a recording as distinguished from the copyright of a song. The copyright of the song encompasses the words and music and is owned by the songwriter or music publisher. The sound recording is the result of recording music, words or other sounds onto a tape, record, CD, etc.

The copyright encompasses what you hear: The artist singing, the musicians playing, the entire production. The sound recording copyright is most often owned by a record label. In the case of DIY/Indies, they often are their own de facto label. They own the copyright if they paid for the production; they can also license its use. The copyright in the musical work (song) itself is owned by the music publisher, which grants the record label a mechanical license to record and distribute.

SYNCH:

Synchronization rights mean you allow your music (work/song) to be used in timed relation to visuals in a film, video, television show, commercial, phone messaging system, or any other type of audio-visual production, for a fee to be specified in a contract between the concerned parties.

Songwriters and publishers then receive synchronization royalties for use of that song when composers, publishers, or music libraries representing their work grant a synch license. Also, if a specific recorded version of that song is being requested for use, then the record company must grant a master use license, too.

THEATRICAL:

Stage plays' use of songs for live performance in a storyline on a stage. Think Broadway, Off-Broadway, West End, etc.

Durden's Down & Dirty Hint & Tip

Making the move to the international market is smart, but it must be done with care and strategy. Do it fast — that is, with no understanding of the country you want to sell into — and you will lose money, hurt your reputation, and could cause an international incident.

International incidents are not good things to start.

MUSIC SUPERVISOR INTERVIEW

Licensing is confusing. But one way to start understanding it is to understand what it is, how it works, and the challenges of those you want to pick your music. Music supervisors' customers are not the songwriters. Songwriters have a product to sell or license to an end user such as movie, TV, ad campaign, etc.

Songs are products. So are socks. Yet we would not confuse the two. A song can be rented (licensed) for varying time periods and have a decades-long shelf life. But have you ever heard of anybody renting socks? No, you haven't. When somebody buys a pair of socks, they wear them out, then buy another pair.

But a song can be sold or rented (licensed) over and over and by various entities, such as for covers (recorded by others), placed in a feature film, and so on.

Unlike socks that are made and sold one time, songs have many earning opportunities that can span decades. That is the long tail of profits contributing to your financial stability. But you can't license what you can't prove you own. Getting to know who a music supervisor (your customer) has to please (his customer), and what his business looks like, will help you to better understand how to have a productive business relationship.

Read an interview of a music supervisor beginning on the next page.

Marc Jackson

Music Supervisor:
MoonLabMusic.com

Q: You indicated your biggest challenge in placing music in films and TV was satisfying the tastes of corporate bosses. How difficult does that make your job?

MARC: Satisfying their tastes isn't the issue as much as getting the direction firsthand. Musical direction being interpreted and then conveyed second-, third-, or sometimes fourth-hand down the chain often leaves out a lot of information that would be useful. My success rate tends to be much higher when I am brought in to interact. Most of the time I can get to what they're wanting because when they aren't necessarily musical, it takes asking the right questions to figure it out. Often what they aren't saying contains more information than what they are saying.

Q: You indicated you are an employee, yet most of your income does not come from music placements. What type of company do you work for? What service or product do they supply and to whom?

MARC: I own a production music company, MoonLab Music, which acts as a music publisher, record label, and music services provider. We work with filmmakers, as well as the studios in movie marketing campaigns. So, we're able to provide more than any one of those entities.

Q: Are filmmakers becoming more or less discerning about the music they put in their films? Other ways to ask this are: Are they more or less concerned with having new music? Or are they okay with using "canned" music from a library even if it only "sort of" works?

MARC: From what I've seen, going with library music for features or shows stems from either budgetary concerns or when a library cue has been used for temp score and becomes the preferred track over time. That's not the rule; it's just what I've seen. To the first part, I don't believe filmmakers are any less discerning about the music in their films at all. Licensing costs for song placement in films runs less expensive than, for example, movie marketing — unless a song is so integral to the story (written into the script), where fees can be quite high. But generally, filmmakers who work with respectable budgets can be creative with songs.

That holds true to a point when adding loads of songs in a film might require negotiating overall rates from a particular publisher. In movie marketing, libraries are used for either budgetary reasons or because they offer tracks designed for marketing, which is notably different than say film score or pop songs.

Q: You indicated one way that you find new music to place in film or TV is by songwriters approaching you. What roles do these songwriters represent? Example: Is the person only songwriter? Or are they also the artist, producer, musician, publisher?

MARC: Indie artists who approach me are typically the songwriter/producer. Often they control their own publishing, but not always.

Q: What issues are there with confirming clear licenses from:

Music libraries?

MARC: Very few issues. They mostly clear master and synch rights and are straightforward to work with.

Music publishers?

MARC: Few issues with publishers. They do a great job providing accurate estimates when needed. And they usually give me great creative choices from their catalogs, which can be quite vast.

Songwriters?

MARC: Songs with loads of writers can be challenging because sometimes just getting ahold of them can be an issue. Particularly writers without publishers or admin people. That can really slow down the clearance process, which is more of a problem when you are in a time crunch, which is often the case.

Online search for song/talent?

MARC: I hate to admit this, but I rarely search for random artists on the interwebs. There is so much music out there that finding great songs in a sea of aspiring unsigned artists isn't the best use of my time, even though in a perfect world I would LOVE to discover the next Imagine Dragons. Bear in mind that even if you find a great song, often the production isn't up to snuff. So that's a tricky venture to be sure.

Q: How often do you have to turn down music because clear license cannot be confirmed?

MARC: Not often. Clearances seem to manage to come together by the 11th hour. Once you reach the parties involved and begin the process, everyone has the same goal. Getting it done and in the show or trailer.

Q: How do you check that those who provide songs have the right to do so?

MARC: Reputable labels, publishers and libraries are a pretty sure bet for establishing that a song isn't being misrepresented. A while back we were using a track from a well-known DJ/artist and were notified by the publisher that an uncleared sample was in the piece. I replaced the sample with one of my own to get the song cleared.

Thankfully, the publisher was the one who alerted us to the problem. For an unsigned artist it *can* be dodgy to ensure proper ownership, but most of the artists I work with know the game pretty well. They want to avoid hot water as much as I do.

Q: You said in the next 10 years you felt the business heading to "hybrids: supervisors more involved with the creative, working in production." In your opinion, what might that look like? And how would content providers pitch you?

MARC: Having the ability to enhance a track, or work with musical stems from the artist to finesse a song while maintaining its integrity, requires the mind of a fellow writer/arranger/producer or having the skill of a very musically inclined music editor in order to do it well.

The term hybrid comes into play when a music supervisor has experience in licensing, finding great music, negotiating terms and all of the typical skills of music supervision, while being a remixer, sound designer, music editor and composer. That's where I want to believe things are headed. But for obvious reasons, if it stays relatively specialized, I'm good with that.

Q: You indicated your business was increasing. What factors have contributed to that?

MARC: The simple answer to that is new media. This has caused synch departments at labels and publishers to expand their synch divisions to service all the original content being created. We'll likely see continued growth in the streaming market space.

SURVIVAL

When Bob Dylan
first began,
he was oblivious
to audience
opinion of him.
He didn't care
because he was
leading that
parade and he knew
that those
who wanted to
follow would.
He was right.

DANGER!

Can sink your small business
and ruin future chances and
careers. Good to know about,
though; there are plenty
who will push you toward
these because it supports
their business models.
BUT DO THEY SUPPORT YOU?

ADVANCE:

A financial payment presented to an artist or band upon signing with a label or publisher.

Advances are **loans against future earnings and must be paid back** to the label or publisher.

In general, advances are not good. If you find yourself with an advance, put it in a separate bank account and do not touch it until it has been earned out and is officially yours.

An advance is not to be confused with a bonus, which is money that does not need to be earned out and is yours from the get-go.

LIVE PERFORMANCE ROYALTIES:

All the performing rights organizations in the U.S. have reporting in place for their writers who are performing their own songs live. Each PRO defines "live" as a performance using live instrumentation (i.e. guitar, keyboard, or some other instrument played onstage by the artist or another person), and *not singing to a track.*

All PROs have information unique to them that they collect from their writer members or affiliates. So check your PRO's current requirements.

You can use these reports to build your venue reporting history that can be used to prove you are *in the business.*

Durden's Down & Dirty Hint & Tip

Beware a Black Swan event. You might not know what the unknown unknowns are, but they exist. Don't be surprised when they show up. Also, don't be surprised when something highly expected does not happen.

AGGREGATOR:

A company that collects content from multiple sources, (re)packages it, and offers it for use by others. In the music business this can emcompass such things as your music included in a catalog of offerings by a third party for streaming, digital download stores, Internet radio, gaming, ringtone providers, ring-back tone services, etc.

I have not yet identified even one digital aggregator (or distributor) whose contract is friendly to creators' I.P. ownership interests.

Therefore, there is only one smart way to use a digital distributor: *Sparingly.*

It is acknowledged you must be able to say your music is on iTunes or a streaming service. That is part of marketing for fans so they will think you are hot stuff.

However, it is *NOT a good business decision* to put ALL or even MOST of your music online with a company that acts as your go-between with international retailers such as iTunes. The reason is that their contracts set you up for losing ownership control of your works.

Furthermore, depending on the aggregator, you could lose control of licensing opportunities. Also, certain aggregators will list your song with a PRO and claim co-publishing ownership status whether or not you agree to it — and the PROs will not say a damn thing about it.

Therefore, it is recommended that you only upload one or two of your songs (and NOT the best ones) of which you do not care if you lose control of their ownership. Call these songs your "Marketing Loss Leaders", use them for bragging rights, but always point fans to direct sales portals you control.

NOT-FOR-PROFIT or NONPROFIT:

An organization that uses surplus revenues to achieve its goals rather than distributing them as profit or dividends. It is permitted to generate surplus revenues, though these must be used by the organization for its self-preservation, expansion, or planned actions. The organization can consist of a combination of controlling members or a board of directors, and paid or volunteer staff that can consist of both management and executives. In many cases, token salaries are used to meet legal requirements for establishing a contract between executive and organization.

Nonprofit or not-for-profit legal status does not mean that the organization intends to lose money, but rather that the organization has no owners and that the funds realized will not be used to benefit any owners. Plus, the methods used to generate revenues may be constrained within a narrow focus.

There is information going around that if an artist sets up a not-for- or non-profit that they can operate without having to report income. That is bad information. Further, setting up such an entity requires a massive amount of extra paperwork and legal filings. Where do you want to spend your time?

If your goal is to avoid Uncle Sam's scrutiny on your bottom line, setting up such an entity will only invite extra scrutiny.

LANCE ALLEN
LanceAllenMusic.com

How to maximize earnings on your catalog and talent.

Q: When you were in 8th grade, you saw a guitar magazine cover that said "How to make a living as a guitarist". That intrigued you, but some years passed. You moved to Nashville in 2002 for recording school and to become a session musician. Did you get much work as a session musician?

LANCE: In college I was one of the go-to guys in the recording classes and for school projects. I tried to break into the session world in Nashville and found it very difficult to get in. There were plenty of musicians just as good as me with years more experience. I could not compete. I was offered a day job working at a music store after college. I took it and put all my efforts into growing the store and teaching guitar lessons.

Q: Then came 2006 and your debut album release. How many copies of the physical product did you get manufactured? How did you sell them? How many did you eventually sell? How long did it take you?

LANCE: I ordered two thousand. Yes, that is a lot, but I was excited to get my first project going. This was before any sites like Kickstarter.com or Indiegogo.com, so the cost was all on me. Most of the CDs I sold on consignment in the music store I worked at. I was a good salesman. I wouldn't order that many now. In fact, there are still 500 or so in my garage. But they are not gathering dust. I use my remaining stock as goodwill gestures in the hopes they will remember me later and spend some money with me.

My focus now is on streaming income, but I plan to have a small inventory of physicals, because when I play shows, people sometimes support you by buying a CD. Better to have them and not need them at every show than to need them and not have them.

Q: So, you were working in a management job and still working on your craft. While out networking at open mics, that job was offered to you by a guy who owned a music store. What did you learn from that experience?

LANCE: At the music store, I learned how to manage a day-to-day business. **The skills and the knowledge I got from the retail business helped me in running my own successful career; so, it wasn't wasted time altogether.** I handled the ordering of music gear from wholesalers, scheduling and hiring employees, and more. I also started a successful eBay store during the time of eBay's peak.

I wasn't happy, but I was scared to just up and quit. After grinding away for eight years, dealing with changing company policies, and finding no room left for professional growth, I finally got the courage to leave the job and go out on my own.

That was one of the best things I could have done.

I was able to treat my customers the way I wanted to. I could make my schedule and charge my rate. I also furthered my business with lessons through Skype and marketed myself through YouTube tutorials. I was able to find a great office space, which was even less than sharing a portion of my revenue from lessons with the store. All in all, it was a great move.

Q: You now have how many albums?

LANCE: Five total, and a handful of singles as digital releases.

Q: Do you still sell physical product?

LANCE: Yes, but not often. When I play at a coffeehouse or house concert, I sell CDs. I usually put out a box and ask people to pay what they wish. Sometimes that works out better than setting a price.

Q: In 2007, you read an article about the founding of the Music Genome Project conceived in 1999 by Will Glaser and Tim Westergren. Glaser, Westergren, and Jon Kraft founded streaming service Pandora. You had a big *aha* moment. Tell us about that.

LANCE: Wasn't so much of an *aha* moment as it was identifying **an exciting and potentially useful** new venue for my music to get out to the public. I had no conception of the service's actually doing well at that time.

Q: How did you monetize Pandora at the beginning?

LANCE: I got money from Pandora organically. Pandora pays its streaming royalties to SoundExchange.com.

Q: SoundExchange.com. You started getting emails from them telling you what?

LANCE: SoundExchange.com was sending me emails saying I needed to sign up, that I may have unclaimed money for my music being streamed. Eventually I got around to signing up for it and, sure enough, I had money waiting on me.

Q: Other than SoundExchange.com, are you registered as a writer and publisher with a performing rights organization?

LANCE: I am with BMI.

Q: Do you release under your own independent label? Do you release using label services from digital distributors?

LANCE: I release music under my name, but not as a label name per se.

Q: Then in 2016, you got on Spotify. Was it your digital distributor who made that happen and you reaped the benefits, or did you have to let Spotify know you were available through a digital distributor?

LANCE: CD Baby was the digital distributor who put my music onto all the streaming platforms. When choosing what platforms to be on, I would select my music to go everywhere, even if it meant free.

Q: Is your music distributed internationally as well as domestically (meaning within the U.S. borders)?

LANCE: Yes, my music is distributed globally.

Q: How do you get paid for those streams?

LANCE: I get paid for streams from the distributor. CD Baby and DisktroKid are my two primary distributors.

Q: How many streaming services are your songs on?

LANCE: Hundreds.

Q: Thinking from the artist's ability to reach out to and market to the listener, what are the differences in the services you are on?

LANCE: It is much easier to find listeners using Spotify than Pandora. It would be a good analogy to liken the Spotify playlist builders as tastemakers along the lines of the DJs from pre-corporate-owned radio station days. So, in effect, I am my own "radio station promoter" or "record company rep".

Q: Can you tell us how you came to understand the available information included in Spotify's platform and the marketing power artists could harness through it?

LANCE: Most of the information I gained was from reading online articles and e-books and making friends in the business, asking questions and so forth. Currently I'm on Spotify's Peaceful Guitar (with three songs); Acoustic

Concentration (two songs); and an Indie playlist called Instrumental Pop, where all my cover songs reside.

Q: How easy is it to purchase the rights to a cover song? How do you go about it?

LANCE: It's very easy. The digital distributor charges a fee to get the license from Harry Fox Agency. Then, the digital distributor deducts the statutory rate to give to the publisher prior to paying me as the artist.

Q: Explain the keyword search available through Spotify.

LANCE: When searching for a playlist, you can just about type in anything related to your style of music, the title of your song, or the emotions that it may evoke. Once you get those results, you find out which your music will best fit in.

Q: You mentioned how you did that. You researched playlist builders and then would reach out to them via direct message through whatever social media they were on or other communication. Can you give us an example of how you could tell that action directly correlated to an uptick in streams?

LANCE: Yes, my first stab at this was finding instrumental pop. I had just recorded a cover song, *Mad World*. I found the playlist quite easily and looked up the creator on Facebook. He accepted my request. I didn't demand anything of him, but I did ask him questions about how he grew his playlist so large, etc. He gave me some pointers that he thought would help. We became friends and now every time I release a cover song it gets on his playlist.

Q: The concept of multiple streams of income is not well known these days. Can you tell us the many ways you are able to monetize your talents and abilities?

LANCE: Yes. Streaming, Fiverr gigs, overdubs, teaching, YouTube, building a core fan group, and consulting. All that stuff. I'm considering putting out a book of music notations of my songs, something people can download. I've even considered selling a course on how to succeed in the streaming world. Still giving that one thought.

Q: But I believe your point is that there is not just one way to earn income from your music.

LANCE: Correct. The music business is hard enough without leaving money on the table.

KEN BONFIELD SAYS: Learn the art of self-promotion. There is no shame in talking about your business.

And your art is your business.

DURDEN SAYS

REAL NUMBERS from Ken Bonfield

Added back catalog to Spotify through CD Baby distribution-only contract: **January 2018**

Wiseman's View original song picked up by a Spotify-curated playlist from 1998 album *Winter Night*: **July 2018**

Streams from July 2018 to mid-November 2018: **3,000,000**

Expected streaming income for this one song: **$13,500±**

Increased market penetration:
Added huge amount of new listeners and fans in a very different demographic. Bulk of Spotify streams have been in the 18-to-35 age group instead of 45+.

SoundExchange.com vs. BMI

Comparing the two agencies, for every *$100* in streaming royalties paid by *SoundExchange.com*, Ken receives *$16.50* in publishing royalties from *BMI*. See next page for details on this. The takeaways here are that one should not expect the PROs alone to deliver income on your songs, also called your intellectual property, and that back catalogs owned free-and-clear can continue earning.

Ken Notes These Points

Earning streams go up and down; length of earning time is not guaranteed.

As an instrumentalist, he does not have to fight the "cult of personality" like vocalists, bands, etc., which have more competitors, making Ken's path to earnings much easier.

Spotify analytics for artists are transparent, thorough, and up to date. **CD Baby** distribution analytics seem clear, though there are a few things unclear.

Pandora and Napster analytics are **cloaked in secrecy.**

Mind the details and the details will pay you.

Transparency. The music business needs more of it. This is Ken's flow of how his intellectual property (song) goes from release to money in his pocket. This is what is in place now. Thank you, Ken, for being so generous with this business info.

We assume you are a true DIY/Indie and are all things: Artist, Publisher, Writer, and Label. If you are not the publisher and/or label, or you share publishing and/or writing/production credits, the flow is still the same but will be more complicated because other entities will be getting paid too, paying you, or needing to be paid.

KEN places
SONG
a/k/a WORK OR INTELLECTUAL PROPERTY

with
CD BABY*

IMPORTANT: NOT Pro LEVEL of MEMBERSHIP

for **DISTRIBUTION SERVICES ONLY.**

AMAZON MUSIC
GOOGLE PLAY
APPLE MUSIC
NAPSTER
(FORMERLY RHAPSODY)
SPOTIFY & PANDORA
CABLE SYSTEMS
SIRIUS
AMONG MANY OTHERS

CD BABY
DISTRIBUTES SONG TO VARIOUS MUSIC SERVICES

RATES PAID FOR MUSIC USE VARY DEPENDING ON WHETHER LISTENER IS FREE OR SUBSCRIBER, AND MANY OTHER VARIABLES.

WHO THEN PAY
ONE OR MORE OF THESE

Then, from 3 months to 1 year later BMI, CD Baby, and SoundExchange.com **PAY**

BMI   **CD BABY**
SOUNDEXCHANGE.COM

BMI pays quarterly if over $250 and splits between Publisher and Writer

CD BABY pays weekly if over $20 and splits between Artist and Label

SoundExchange.com pays monthly if over $250 and splits between Artist and Label

KEN

for FOUR income categories:
Writer. Publisher. Label. Artist.

* There are other digital aggregators and performing rights societies and organizations, and thousands of outlets, but we are only using Ken's vendors and PROs here to keep it simple.

THIS CHART DOES NOT INCLUDE KEN'S RETAIL SALES OF PHYSICAL PRODUCT OR DOWNLOADS.

SURVIVAL

When it comes to
audiences, the
only thing under
your control is
your performance.
Focus on what
you can control.
Love your audience.
Share with them.
Invite them into
your world.

DURDEN'S DOWN & DIRTY DISPATCHES

DURDEN'S DOWN & DIRTY
OPEN LETTER TO
THE HONORABLE ALISON J. NATHAN
CONCERNING THE
FERRICK et al v. SPOTIFY USA INC.
CLASS-ACTION LAWSUIT

Letter to the Honorable Alison J. Nathan
Re: Ferrick v. Spotify USA Inc.,
No. 1:16-cv-8412 (AJN)

Honorable Alison J. Nathan
Courtroom 906
United States District Court for the
Southern District of New York,
Thurgood Marshall United States Courthouse
40 Foley Square
New York, NY 10007

Wednesday, September 20, 2017

Dear Honorable Alison J. Nathan,

According to the website www.SpotifyPublishingSettlement.com, the fairness of *Ferrick v. Spotify USA Inc.* is due to be heard/decided by you on December 1, 2017.

This letter will establish that the proposed settlement is **injurious** to music content creators, is **unfair** on its face, and will set a legal precedent for **further destruction of copyright protections** for all content creators whether in music, books, art, etc.

As a songwriter and publisher, I have chosen never to release music through any digital aggregator or digital distributor. The two songs I have registered as a copyright owner have never been released publicly by me or my co-writer. The reasons for this decision are:

1. Digital aggregators/distributors are notorious for remastering and assigning their own ISRC.
2. Digital aggregators/distributors are sloppy in their

recordkeeping and often assign the same ISRC to five or more musical works by different artists.

3. Digital aggregators/distributors claim co-publisher ownership status with songwriters when registering the work with ASCAP, BMI, or SESAC (Performing Rights Organizations, or PROs).

    a. This goes against their own Terms of Service but has not stopped them.

    b. The PROs know of this practice and do not speak up to the digital aggregators/distributors, thus allowing the money flow to be even murkier.

Since I have never employed the services of a digital aggregator / distributor, and the only way to get onto Spotify is to have uploaded a digital file to a service of this sort for distribution to such an outlet, you can see that when I received two postcards in the mail telling me of the above referenced lawsuit I was not sure why I was included.

This lawsuit looks good on its face, but when one has a deeper understanding of the forces at play and the end goals of those forces, then one is obliged to look deeper. This is what I did and I quickly became concerned.

Having received many class action notices in my lifetime, they've always had two options: (1) Do nothing and include yourself or (2) let them know if you want to be excluded. Easy and clear.

Ferrick v. Spotify USA Inc. has three weasel-word options, each couched in such a way that no matter what happens, Spotify USA Inc. will have nothing more to pay to content creators than the $43.45 million.

Option One: Include yourself by filling out the claim
                form and give up all future rights to sue
                Spotify for infringement. *This means they
                can use the same song again and owe
                nothing to the owners.*
Option Two: Exclude yourself by telling them every
                song for which you have filed a
                copyright registration.
Option Three: Do nothing and you still give up all
                future rights to sue for infringement.
                This speaks for itself.

What is clear is that **this settlement seeks to represent all
holders of copyrights of music** *whether or not that music has
ever been released.*

Spotify is aiming to pay in advance for any copyright
infringement of songs they may use in the future, thus the three
options above. This settlement is attempting to set up Spotify
with a "get out of copyright jail free" option.

That is, Spotify will never have to pay any fines required by the
copyright laws because they will have set up this fund to settle
— at mere fractions of a penny on the dollar — for stealing
rightfully owned intellectual property from content creators,
*many of whom have chosen never to do business with Spotify in
the first place* and who are being asked now to give up rights to
any future action when Spotify steals their songs again.
I asked the Settlement Administrator where Spotify got their
information so they would know where to send the postcards.
The Administrator said they got it all from Copyright.gov.

Why are all copyright holders of songs — *including those with songs that have not been released for distribution or sale* — receiving demands to include or exclude themselves in this Spotify lawsuit? There is a more solid technique that will protect content creators without having to blanket the entire U.S. with predatory and burdensome demands.

Simply require Spotify to make *their entire playlist* available online. It should minimally include the following information they have about any song, namely:

Song title;
publisher (if known);
artist (if known);
writers (if known).

Then let everybody who has put songs out for the public go check the website and claim their song by then providing proof by which they can then include themselves in the lawsuit settlement.

Of course, this solution assumes Spotify has only been getting songs for their playlist through digital aggregators, direct license from administrators of large catalogs, publishers, and labels. If Spotify is getting music through illegal means, then this lawsuit is even more evil. In fact, given how this lawsuit is worded, I am inclined to think it, thus the blanket demands mitigating future fines.

However, contrary to popular opinion and Google / Alphabet's newest scheme to the contrary, copyright registration of and by itself is not required to own your own content nor is it proof of an ownership stake in a work. There are over 10 individual pieces required to establish a clear license of a song for it to be placed in a movie or used in an ad campaign. These proofs are the *basis of the right* to copyright.

Copyright trolls know most people don't know this; they take advantage of that gap in knowledge. Google's copyright trolling started with books in the late 1990s and early 2000s. At the time, I sent Google a letter telling them they do not have a right to scan my book, I do not give permission, and they better not cut me out of sales of my own product. For years Google has been attempting to become the biggest copyright troll of all time. Ask Ryan Fox, an attorney with the Authors Guild, Inc. — website is authorsguild.org — just how nasty this fight is continuing to get because Google's goals have not changed.

Even major labels, publishers, and other catalog administrators do a sloppy job of paperwork — some say this is by design. I reference here Warner Music Group's copyright claim to the *Happy Birthday* song. They never owned it, but Warner simply told everybody they did and collected royalties for 60 years. *It took 60 years to have someone finally challenge them.* Warner was ordered to pay millions in damages.

To assume Spotify's simplistic settlement arrangement is fair to victims is absurd on its face. If the settlement pot they've established is divided by even one million copyrighted songs that somehow manage to include themselves in the lawsuit, the fine per song is a mere $43.45 — and that's if the years-long appeals are lost. It takes much more than $43.45 to write, record, produce, legally protect and defend, and market a song.

All music copyright holders — a/k/a Spotify victims — are being forced to give the thief a "get out of copyright jail free" card *and* being told to leave the door open so the thief can come back.

For the sake of all copyright holders both now and in the future who want to make money — if not a living — from their creations, I implore you not to allow this settlement to go through. Please do not approve it.

As it sits, this settlement isn't fair and it isn't right.

Your Honor, *you* are the one standing between millions of creatives and their rights as citizens of the United States. *You* are the one standing between the bullies holding works as hostage and the victims. I and millions of other creators pray you have the courage and wisdom to do the right thing.

Sincerely,

Angela K. Durden

UPDATE:

It is my belief this letter, among other communications from interested parties, may have helped the judge to extend her judgment period, but for reasons unknown to me, as of the writing of this book the judge ruled in favor of letting the class-action settlement proceed as indicated.

However, several interested parties have petitioned the court not to finalize it yet. I thank these individuals and companies for fighting the fine fight against an obvious property grab.

IF YOU WANT A COPY OF THE ORIGINAL LETTER IN PDF FORM, PLEASE EMAIL ME AT:

angeladurden@msn.com

I will send it to you if you ask for it.
No charge.

HOW & WHEN TO USE A PERFORMING RIGHTS ORGANIZATION

Only join a performing rights organization such as ASCAP, BMI, and/or SESAC as a writer and/or publisher, and list only mastered songs, if your works:

- are being placed in films, TV, etc.;
- are being sold in the retail marketplace;
- are under full or partial control of another publisher;
- might be released without your knowledge;
- are on streaming services (with or without your permission);
- are being played on terrestrial radio;
- have been distributed by digital aggregators such as TuneCore and CD Baby, among others.

Or if you:
- aren't the only one on the split sheet;
- do not trust your producer or other production team members.

Durden's Down & Dirty Hint & Tip

Do you think of yourself as only a singer or musician? Why aren't you upping the investment in your career by writing, licensing, and publishing? Hmmmm?

Lots of effort has gone into it, but the MMA won't work.

The overview of the Music Modernization Act (MMA) has two parts. One: What will be done away with, and two: What will take those places.

On its face, the MMA looks good. But execution of it is problematic. In other words, much easier said than done.

As the inventor of an easy-to-use service that systematically collected and validated ownership information in a completely transparent fashion (My Digital Catalog, out of business as a SaaS on 12/31/2017), I know of what I speak. Not trying to be a downer, simply a realist, so let me tell you why this new legislation is not going to work.

The bill says it will have all digital services fund a Mechanical Licensing Collective (MLC), which will grant them blanket mechanical licenses for interactive streaming and digital downloads of musical works.

Q: How will the funding be distributed? If it is done now like all blanket licenses, then the little guy is cheated. In other words, BOHICA. [Bend Over. Here It Comes Again.]

Q: Who will govern the MLC? The MMA says publishers and self-published songwriters. Mark my words, it will be run by the likes of Sony/ATV and Warner Music Group. Any self-published songwriter involved in the governance will be a token and will have no real say-so.

It gets worse. The MLC is to address the challenges digital services face when attempting to match songwriters and publishers with recordings played on streaming services. Has anybody asked SoundExchange.com and their new Notice of Intention of Use (NOI) lookup about how that is going with the 60 million address unknowns?

I went to the SXWorks and looked up a friend of mine. One of his songs came up as being licensed by Google for streaming. He was never informed of it and I can guarantee he takes care of his paperwork.

Still, most songwriters, producers, and artists — willy-nilly — upload their music to digital distributors who then play fast and loose with ownership data and money streams. Most songwriters, producers, and artists have not taken the time to document their ownership stake in any song they have uploaded.

Which brings us to the next thing the MMA would do: Provide a transparent and publicly accessible database housing song ownership information. Sounds good. But —

Who will input these millions of bits of ownership information? How will ownership information be validated?

The answer to the latter is, it won't be.

The answer to the former is, please oh please don't let it be ASCAP, BMI, SESAC, or any of the digital distributors because they have already cheated it up, thank you very much. Not that the cheat-up is completely their fault, but I've written about that in the past and won't address it here.

Durden's Down & Dirty Hint & Tip

Beware the Flim-Flam Man. The one who talks fast and always has a pie-in-the-sky answer and makes the big promises to get you X for $$$. They are lying or stupid. Neither is good.

Durden's Down & Dirty Hint & Tip

PROs and other collection agencies' efforts on your behalf are only as good their internal systems *and your ability to check up on them.* Keep separate records of your songs' ownership information.

Gnawing their own leg, part deux: "Property rights be damned!" say The Bigs, The Majors, and Tech Giants.

So, you think you own your intellectual property and can license it as you please?

Think again. Seems one Rep. Jim Sensenbrenner (R-WI) wants to help The Bigs, The Majors, and all those poor put-upon Tech Giants cheat creators.

An article on MusicTech.Solutions does a great job of explaining the backstory details of the bill. But let me summarize this situation for you.

The Bigs, The Majors, and Tech Giants (like Twitter, Google/Alphabet, Facebook, CD Baby, etc.) want to not only use your stuff for free, they want to be able to resell it without paying you for your contribution.

The Bigs, The Majors, and Tech Giants are only rich on paper. They have no real money. If they did they wouldn't be laying off employees who handle the licensing paperwork and royalty tracking.

Stockholders are getting ready to get a couple of proverbial dried corncobs shoved up their wallets as creators take their works off Tech Giant distribution portals and go direct-to-fan (including physical sales).

Politicians are rolling over to have their tummies tickled by The Bigs, The Majors, and the poor put-upon Tech Giants.

With a big push from The Recording Academy, both Louisiana and Georgia passed state bills to give tax credits pushing music business economic development initiatives. That these bills only benefit larger touring acts is their Achilles' heel. But the bigger point is:

With the passage of this copyright-protection-gutting bill, there will be no large touring acts, so where will those economic development bills be then, huh?

BOHICA, Part Deux: Hey, PROs —
You know your business is over, right?

If you are a rights owner of music compositions, then you should have questions. I know I do.

According to an article on Bloomberg.com, it looks like Facebook is making blanket license deals with The Majors and The Bigs. Which they can do. Nothing illegal about that. But hey, ASCAP, BMI, and SESAC:

Are you feeling the burn from being cut out? How do you feel about your businesses being deemed irrelevant?

"Music owners have been negotiating with Facebook for months in search of a solution, and Facebook has promised to build a system to identify and tag music that infringes copyrights," Bloomberg reports.

Does this sound like in the Great Copyright Database Control Race and Facebook is whipping its pony to get past Google/Alphabet's doped horse?

From Bloomberg: "While Facebook can still pursue professional music videos, the company chose to prioritize clearing user-generated material."

Is Facebook setting themselves up as a hybrid? Part performing rights organization accusing deep pockets of infringement and chasing them, and part protective Big Brother looking after their "slow" siblings?

Further from Bloomberg: "Music industry executives also hope licensing songs for user-generated video on Facebook will place greater pressure on YouTube to behave."

Don't The Bigs, The Majors, and Tech Giants understand they are being forced to gnaw on their own legs by DIY/Indies who are opting out of those systems?

Still gnawing on their own leg: Google uses dead-of-night legislation as force of law to flat-out steal from and bankrupt songwriters.

If you have any doubt that copyright is under attack around the world, look no further than Alphabet's latest aggression on content creators via Google. Years ago when Google started scanning in books without publisher or author permissions and making those works available online, author organizations fought back with a vengeance. I was part of that fight.

Google backed down, but they didn't change their mind: They believe they have a right to go into your barn and steal your horses, and let others use them without paying you.

You've heard me (and others like the Content Creators Coalition) saying it for several years now.

The most recent article about these attacks on rights came through an article entitled "The Shiv Act" written by Chris Castle wherein he says:

> "Whatever the discussions have been in the music community about the need for a 'global rights database', nobody ever said 'And what we really need is a "use it or lose it" system that allows Big Tech to question every lawsuit based on whether a work was registered under the right title by the right people at the right time….'
> and so on and so on and so on.

"This legislation has all kinds of potential international implications as did the taxpayer debacle known as the Fairness In Music Licensing Act, which benefited MIC Coalition members but has cost the U.S. taxpayer millions of dollars as a result of treaty violations.

"The MIC Coalition is back with more crony capitalism asking for another taxpayer funded even safer harbor, a legislated knife to stick in the backs of songwriters and artists."

In 2018, the European Union fined Google $2.7 billion for nasty shenanigans toward businesses, and what are songwriters but small businesses that are now being attacked and the rights to their digital assets stolen?

You want to know who's in bed with Google on this? You'll have to look no further than The Majors and The Bigs in every country.

It's time the songwriters fought back:

- Go DIY/Indie all the way.
- Don't put whole songs out for free listening unless it is a loss-leader promotion.
- Sign up with aggregators only for limited services.
- Go direct-to-fan.
- And if need be, take your music offline completely because according to Google, if it goes online and you haven't registered it in a special database that you will never be able to access or will never be told how to find, then you are well and truly...

CHEATED.

I would say yay for ASCAP except for...

A recent press release about ASCAP makes out like that performing rights organization is looking after the rights of their content owners by suing 10 live performance venues for not purchasing a blanket license. The article was self-serving and woefully lacking in proper information such as:

First: Why did these 10 venues stop paying?

Second: Were the venues being dinged even when bands played their own original music live? No infringement there, so what's the problem?

Third: ASCAP knows about and allows a worse assault on songwriters' royalties: It allows to go unchallenged CD Baby's unlawful claim to original publisher status on songs CD Baby lists on behalf of their Pro customers. Nowhere in CD Baby's contract does it say there is a business relationship between CD Baby and their customer.

What does this mean?

CD Baby emphatically states the contract between them and their customer expressly limits the relationship to independent contractor.

Claiming original publisher status when listing songs means CD Baby is now claiming to be in business with everybody they are performing that service for.

CD Baby knows their contract says they will only be Admin for their Pro client.

Industrywide, Catalog Admins get a percentage fee for handling paperwork, but Admins do not *own any part of the copyright in the song, which is what being a co-publisher means.*

Admins handle paperwork for licensing and placements. If they make a sweet deal for their client, their take is higher, but the percentage category remains the same whether it is as independent contractor or vendor.

If you are an ASCAP member and you have a Pro account with CD Baby, you should log in to your ASCAP member portal and see if CD Baby has claimed they own half of the publishing of any of your songs.

I would love to hear what you find out about your catalog's rights ownership.

In the meantime, ASCAP's article about hunting down 10 restaurants — claiming copyright infringement — is self-serving on their part since they refuse to take CD Baby to task for the much larger egregious action of taking half the publishing ownership of their Pro customers.

ASCAP takes the word of the much larger digital aggregator when they say their contract allows them to do it, even though, upon reading the entire contract, it is beyond clear CD Baby is not allowed.

I repeatedly contacted ASCAP about this on behalf of a particular client who wanted to know what was going on with his catalog.

On the following pages you will see *part* of the email exchange between me and ASCAP on behalf of my client.
[I have redacted email addresses and the client's name.]

From: ASCAP Employee Candace
To: [Client Name Redacted]

CD Baby maintains their claim to publisher status.

Sincerely,
ASCAP Employee Candace

From: Angela K. Durden
To: ASCAP Employee Candace

Good afternoon, Candace.

[Client Name Redacted] forwarded me the communication chain from you to him.

We are very distressed about CD Baby Alpha Music maintaining their claim to co-publisher status. That they are claiming to be in a co-owner relationship with one of their customers goes completely against their own terms of service contract as quoted here:

20. General Provisions:
(a) Relationship of the Parties. The parties hereto agree and acknowledge that the relationship between them **is that of independent contractors. This Agreement shall not be deemed to create an agency, partnership or joint venture between you and CD Baby,** and CD Baby shall not have a fiduciary obligation to you as a result of your entering into this Agreement.

As you can see from very specific language, they are prohibited from going into mutual business with their customers and limits their actions to independent contractor, which capacity they have as Administrator. Mr. [Client Name Redacted] does not dispute this. (For your convenience, I have attached the entire TOS from CD Baby for your review.)

Previous to contacting ASCAP, Mr. [Client Name Redacted] asked CD Baby to remove CD Baby Alpha Music as co-publisher, rescinding their claim to ownership status. Their answer was that they are "required" to be a co-publisher in order to receive his royalties.

This is flatly a false premise.

As ASCAP is very well aware, many administrators collect and distribute all day long without claiming to own half of what they represent. They do this for a fee. CD Baby Alpha Music is receiving fees as an administrator. At no time has Mr. [Client Name Redacted] granted half of his catalog's earnings as a co-rightsholder to CD Baby or CD Baby Alpha Music.

We view CD Baby and CD Baby Alpha Music's actions in this regard to be predatory and illegal.

Our question to ASCAP is this: As the premier performing rights organization in the United States, and as an organization that is always "on the Hill" advocating for songwriters' rights, the one that says it is member-run, and which attracts its members with promises of supporting those rights, **how can ASCAP advocate on behalf of Mr. [Client Name Redacted] to protect his property from this multinational corporation taking his stuff?**

It has also come to our attention that this is standard operating procedure with CD Baby Alpha Music claiming half of their Pro customers' publishing. I believe that, since CD Baby Alpha Music must be a publisher member of ASCAP in order to list themselves with the E (Original

Publisher) designation, it is possible that ASCAP is finding themselves in a sticky situation.

How can ASCAP protect their members from another of their members when a *pattern of theft has been demonstrated by another large member*?

I do not envy ASCAP's position at this time. Furthermore, it is not our intention of "fixing the whole CD Baby Alpha Music problem."

Mr. [Client Name Redacted] simply wants *his* catalog to be free of CD Baby Alpha Music's ownership claims as original publisher.

I certainly hope you are the one that can have that conversation with someone at CD Baby Alpha Music who can authoritatively make the needed changes on Mr. [Client Name Redacted] behalf. Otherwise, I hope you can please forward this entire email including the member agreement attached to someone who can suggest to CD Baby Alpha Music that taking the high road in this instance is in the best interests of themselves, Mr. [Client Name Redacted], and ASCAP.

Thanking you much for your kind attention to this matter,

angela | k | durden
404.358.0951 direct

From: Angela K. Durden
To: ASCAP Employee Candace

Good afternoon, Candace.

It's has been over a month since I sent the email below stating our position concerning CD Baby Alpha Music's claim to ownership status of Mr. [Client Name Redacted] works. Mr. [Client Name Redacted] nor I have received any reply to this. His ASCAP catalog listings do not show that CD Baby Alpha Music has made any changes to that claim.

Who at ASCAP can handle this?

Thank you,

angela | k | durden
404.358.0951 direct

FOLLOW-UP
From: Angela K. Durden
To: ASCAP Employee Alex

Good afternoon, Alex.

As per your instructions to bring you up to speed so you could further research the situation, please see the email chain below which contains the information pertinent to your research. I have emailed [Candace] several times since then and received no reply and have called and left a message once.

I have copied your member, Mr. [Client Name Redacted], on this email.

We are looking forward to hearing from you.

Sending warm regards to you,

angela | k | durden
404.358.0951 direct

ASCAP ceased returning my phone calls and answering my emails. As of this writing (2018) — over two years after beginning inquiries — Mr. [Client Name Redacted] has still not received any other word from CD Baby or ASCAP about this matter. Rightful ownership of his works is still in limbo.

2017: The Year the Music Business Died

I've been saying it for quite some time and been laughed at for my troubles. Yet, I read and think and compare and question. I've said it and my readers have all heard me say it:

**"If you want your money,
go direct-to-fan, boys and girls."**

2017 is the year the plug was pulled on the digital distribution model in which everybody including major and small labels, major and small publishers, the DIY community, all performing rights organizations, and many a publicly traded company and investment group put their hopes for a profitable balance sheet. Let me give you the short 4-1-1:

DIY distributors such as, but not limited to, CD Baby, DistroKid, TuneCore, Symphonic, OneRPM, Ditto, Horus, RouteNote, MondoTunes, ReverbNation — frankly all the others, too, because I've been reading their contracts — have put artists' and songwriters' royalties into limbo. How have they done that?

It's called The Blame Game.

Distributors' fingers point to Pandora, who points to Labels, who point to Publishers, who point to PROs, all the while creators' money mysteriously floats around the world from one country to the next, hiding behind fake confidentiality agreements creators don't know exist.

The Bigs and The Majors have lost track of the money, y'all.

Making the distribution system so complicated that the creators of the music cannot figure how they are getting cheated, The Bigs and The Majors ended up outsmarting themselves. Yes, while giving the old "eff you" to the creators, they ending up effing themselves.

The more they lost control, the tighter they squeezed. We know this from the consolidations in the business, making all but a very few of these companies publicly traded, who had better meet quarterly stockholder performance expectations — or else.

Do you create music? Do you want people to hear it?

Then put only one or two songs into the digital distribution arena. Think of those songs as loss leaders. Think of them as your marketing tool.

But then point them to you and sell...

Direct-to-fan.

You'll get your money faster (Fan buys. You get money!) and you'll have a better chance of retaining ownership of the rights to that music, too.

Instead of realizing their
business model is dead,
The Bigs, The Majors, and Tech Giants
attempt to entice new business
from creatives and DIY/Indies
by sneakier methods,
ever more obtuse contracts,
and self-destructive behavior.
They often manage to do this
through duped sub-distributors.

At the same time, business is
so bad they reduce workforces and
consolidate the industry into huge
slow-moving reactive monopolies
while taking credit for
massive industry growth.

This massive industry growth
is nothing but a house of cards
waiting on a stiff wind to blow.

They buy and sell
each other into oblivion.

ALL THIS AFFECTS YOUR ABILITY TO
SELL YOUR PRODUCT IF YOU
RELY SOLELY ON THEM.

Music Streaming Services' Conundrum

Since the songwriter is the very last to get paid, where's the money for the songwriter? The music streaming services' conundrum is complicated.

On the one hand, everybody thinks this business model is awesome. Easy access to distribution for artists makes it attractive. See, say the streamers, we can deliver millions of ears and eyeballs.

Won't cost you a thing, they say.

We'll even pay you, they promise.

On the other hand, as streamers dance the light fandango, their balance sheets turn from black to a whiter shade of pale.

"After years of trading physical dollars for digital dimes, the music industry is finally seeing a payoff. Subscriptions to streaming music services jumped about 50 percent in 2016, topping 92 million. For the first time since the heyday of CDs, revenue for the largest record labels is consistently rising. But things don't look as bright for the streaming companies driving this revival."
Bloomberg Businessweek, Technology
January 9-January 15, 2017

Can we really say these 92 million are unique customers since many people have more than one music streaming service subscription?

I don't think we can.

There are only so many hours in the day that people listen. Removing time-limited exclusive deals from the mix, everybody seems to have most of the same songs. Since music streaming is not dependent on a local market, where's the advantage?

This is the music streaming services' conundrum in action.

Part of what drove the 2016 uptick in subscriptions was the embedding of the technology in new cars. Giving it away and hoping new owners will continue the service is, at best, a gamble. Further, we know that of these 92 million subscriptions, most are not paid. Freemium versions get their revenue by attracting eyeballs to ads. Nobody believes the eyeball count anymore.

Especially after the Facebook video debacle of 2016.

Facebook admitted that for over two years their video tracking algorithm had been vastly inflating how long video display ads were watched. "Oops, our bad" does not inspire confidence. Upshot? Freemium versions' ad revenue is way down.

So where's the profit? There isn't any.

The big question now becomes: How will content creators make money on their creations if they continue to push their product into losing platforms and distribution systems? Consider these facts: Spotify pays 70% of its revenue to publishers and labels, while continuing to swallow huge losses year after year. Investors are skittish.

Pandora has never made a profit and is looking to raise their subscription rates while deploying technology from a struggling company they bought somewhere around 2016.

Rhapsody and Deezer are walking a mile in Spotify and Pandora's shoes; iHeartRadio filed for bankruptcy in 2018.

Apple, Amazon, and Google push out fun, free, and helpful services that are simply loss leaders used to attract customers for other stuff they want to sell for other businesses. In other words: They attract eyeballs.

SoundCloud, bless their hearts, truly trying to do the right thing for artists and songwriters, took too long to clean up their I.P. ownership mosh pit and launch. (In hopes of finding a cash cow, Twitter invested $70 million in SoundCloud — and lost $66.4 million.)

In all cases, everybody is fighting over the same customers and offering the same product. Songwriters are denied direct access to the customers and asked to be happy with just a few pennies thrown their way.

I came from outside of the music business, eyes fresh. Wanting to learn, I questioned everything but was not liking what I heard. After more research with certain conclusions reached, and pointing out what was needed to ensure protections of I.P. data were put in place at the grassroots level, I was poo-poohed and made fun of by many industry insiders.

In some instances I have become *persona non grata,* to be avoided at all costs.

But then highly respected business magazines, Forbes and Bloomberg among others, began writing articles pretty much rubber-stamping everything I had already concluded. **That's when I had to ask myself:**

Since the songwriter is the very last to get paid, where's the money for the songwriter?

At this time, precious few are making a living placing their original music. Making tracking impossible are music placement services playing games with titling. Major labels no longer make deals with fresh talent.

They choose to work with those they have slaving under onerous contracts.

Songwriters must protect themselves.

Songwriters must be choosy with whom they work and collaborate if they expect to sell their music and protect the long tail of their earnings.

So, listen. When I tell you that I pay attention to the basis of the deal. When I say I don't make deals with chuckleheads. When I tell you I'm actively searching for a better way to make money from my creations.

I expect others are doing the same.

Bless his little ol' heart:
Reznor, Apple, and YouTube

Uh, oh. I'm getting ready to say *it*. What is *it*, you ask? In New Jersey, *it* would be if I called Trent Reznor a *boombot*.

In the South we say, "Oh, buhLESS hizz li'l ol' heart." And we would pat him on the hand and ask, "Dahlin', would you like a suhweet tea with that opinion?"

It all means the same thing though. Mr. Reznor hasn't a clue about what is really happening in the music business. I invite him to visit the little people who are out there trying to navigate the convoluted mess that he's been successful in — with the help of a major label, that is.

Mr. Reznor is quoted on Hypebot.com as saying:

"…YouTube's business…is built on the backs of free, stolen content…. I think any free-tiered service is not fair….We're [Apple] trying to build a platform that provides an alternative – where you can get paid and an artist can control where their [content] goes."

Hypebot.com posted this from a Google exec: "The overwhelming majority of labels and publishers have licensing agreements in place with YouTube….Today the revenue from fan uploaded content accounts for roughly 50 percent of the music industry's YouTube revenue. Any assertion that this content is largely unlicensed is false. To date, we have paid out over $3 billion to the music industry – and that number is growing year on year."

But let's address two points.

One: Free-tiered. Look, YouTube does not charge me any money to upload my content. I decide how it can be used. If I want to monetize it, then YouTube and I make another deal. In the meantime, I am free to point to my video on my channel at no charge, can remove it when I want, and they help with anyone using it without my permission. I call that a win-win situation for those of us just getting started.

Two: Other than the major labels who may have independent licensing deals with Apple, Mr. Reznor has no idea where Apple gets most of their music from. I shall tell him. From the digital aggregators, most of whom's user contracts are nothing short of criminal.

So, Trent, stop reading from the script that Apple has written for you. Stop drinking their Kool-Aid. And give me a call because, Baby, Sweetie, Honey Chile, Sugar Bunch, I'll tell you what you are missing and how you are supporting systems and processes that are cheating the DIY/Indie. You're a smart fella, you'll figure out how to get in touch.

These [READER] comments were posted on Linkedin after this article ran.
Lee

Interesting... similar to Prince...he was once at the forefront of championing the Internet even being pioneering with it, but once they realized money was not rolling in as much from his new releases, [he was] suddenly the enemy. Once [you] get rich it would appear all [you] want to do is be even richer.

Artists rights need addressing on a very basic ground level (i.e. so people realize at some point if they don't pay for music they won't get much good stuff for much longer — (same with fiIm) — and the attitude towards art and artists has to change...Apple (despite user friendly equipment) are no saviours. Guess this means he won't be soundtracking the youtube inventor's movie then. ;-)

{READER] comment
William Ferguson
CEO/Founder Nova Media Group US, Artist/Producer

I agree with you up to a point — there really wasn't any way for artists like Prince or Trent Reznor to predict how the Internet would impact royalties when the idea of digital music distribution got off the ground.

At the time it seemed like a great idea. Hell, even I was all for it. It meant that an Indie like me was granted access to a worldwide market in which I could sidestep the industry altogether, blaze my own trail and live by my own rules.

It didn't turn out to be the great equalizer we all were promised and hoped it would.

[READER] comment
Lee in reply to William Ferguson

William Ferguson — too true on the independent side of things, but I can't help but think the way big business perverted social media and turned it into an impersonal promotion device (or even worse, a totally considered, cynical one!) rather than a genuine channel to artists, combined with the influx of hobbyist musicians turning the net into a sea of musicians good and bad, but more importantly blurring the lines between 'serious' and 'for fun in spare time' type musicians. Another consequence of technology...don't get me wrong, I think everyone should and can do music but even at the start of this century, there were still a set of processes / hurdles / stages mapped out for a band/act etc., to get from [A-to-B] in a career, hard as those may have been.

In the last 10 years or so, it's become so wide even the most adventurous...listener would be daunted enough by the sea of music in front of them to rely on media with corporate interests for their tastes.

Regarding those acts, I get what you mean entirely, but it's also the privilege of the millionaire to even want to charge for music these days, when in actual fact, they are the ones who could afford to give it away...while we have to fight tooth and nail to get people to pay enough attention to download a free song let alone charge them for it.

Essentially these acts are part of the machine whether they or we want to admit or like it. It's how they got their wealth but now that this is the way we share music/find it etc, they are [against] it to the point of removing someone covering or remixing their song from the net — despite the fact that because of audience reticence to new/unfamiliar songs, these are some of the only ways of getting noticed/fans etc.

I believe music is worth paying for but —

1. People have been overcharged (I have 1000s of CDs I paid £15 for that are now worth 20p each) and
2. I'm a bit more concerned for the starving musicians of the future than the millionaire ones of the past. I love both Trent and Prince and owe them both a lot in terms of inspiration but as someone who spent a small fortune on them, I get angry when I think they may be scuppering the futures of the people they used to be.

All the best to you in your career though. Hope you find ways to navigate this era! :-)

BLACK HOLE OF DIGITAL DESPAIR: THE DMCA

The writers of the DMCA had good intentions, but they themselves did not understand the nature of intellectual property rights. Therefore, the solution was punitive, even to rights owners.

Good luck ever seeing this reversed in Congress.

DMCA: Digital Millennium Copyright Act

A summary in all its gory detail can be found here:
en.wikipedia.org/wiki/Digital_Millennium_Copyright_Act

The DMCA was out of date exactly one day after President Bill Clinton signed it into law. The DMCA is so rigid that it has not been able to keep up with the flood of new material released into the wild by millions of songwriters, nor new technology.

The DMCA criminalizes production and dissemination of technology, devices, or services intended to circumvent digital rights management that controls access to copyrighted works.

The mere act of circumventing an access control *whether or not* there is actual copyright infringement is, technically speaking, a criminal act.

With stiff penalties, the DMCA increases the consequences for copyright infringement on the Internet yet provides no real solution to the problem of theft or piracy in any form. It has proven nearly impossible for all parties to comply with.

Creatives are hardest hit.

BEWARE ADVANCES

If you need the money so badly that you are willing to sign away your rights and take a big advance, then you have already lost any marketplace advantage you thought you had and thrown away any future earnings. Don't believe me? Just ask some of the major acts who made that decision early in their careers and came to rue it: Chicago, Prince, The Beatles, and other songwriters and bands.

In other words, don't be a sucker and spend the advance money immediately. Wait to see if you will have to pay it back. You'll thank me later.

BEWARE THE UNSEEN PIT OF LOST PROFIT FROM CONTROLLED COMPOSITION CLAUSES

If you are releasing your own music on your own label under your own publishing company imprint, you do not need to worry about controlled composition clauses.

If you place a song with an artist and deal with their publishing company and/or other publishing companies, you will definitely want to pay attention to this clause.

HAVE AN ATTORNEY REVIEW the contract before you sign or make any promises. It's called negotiation.

HARRY FOX AGENCY (HFA)

I question HFA's effectiveness. In a novel I wrote, I wanted to completely quote lyrics to a popular song by Bread from the early 1970s. To license the print rights for those lyrics and make sure the writers and publishers got paid for their intellectual property, I first looked at the repertories of the U.S. performing rights organizations (PROs) to search for the song. Found it at ASCAP, who said to talk to HFA. I went to HFA. They said they didn't handle print rights, go to the PRO or publisher.

I went back to the PRO and the information for the publisher was out of date.

As of the time of this writing, I have not yet been able to license the print rights to the lyrics even though I have wanted to pay for those rights.

The system is set up only to serve a narrow niche: The Majors and The Bigs. They know it. There is nothing wrong with that, but don't waste your time trying to get HFA to service your business needs.

SALES AND PLAYS REPORTING AGENCIES

Nielsen BDS makes it almost impossible for individuals to have their songs counted. The reason is that it's a lot of paperwork and they are a for-profit company servicing those who can afford their services.

DIY/Indies usually cannot afford their fees. Save your time and don't try to submit. Instead, focus on growing direct sales and building your fan base.

360 DEALS:
PUBLISHERS, LABELS, AND YOU

360 deals may not be a bad thing, but do not take the label or publisher's word that one will be good for you.

One hour of entertainment attorney time can drastically increase opportunities for more profit from your brand and product. Don't be cheap because if you are, you cheat yourself — and your collaborators.

THE DIRTY DEALS OF
DIGITAL DISTRIBUTORS

There are several popular and widely used aggregators (digital distributors) who will get your songs and albums onto streaming services and into iTunes, etc. These act as high-volume managers that assign ISRCs, but they keep sloppy records so that one ISRC is being assigned to more than one version of a song, as well as being assigned to other songs that are not associated with the original rights holder and/or artist.

This completely messes up the accuracy of the process of tracking sales and paying royalties as well as muddies the ownership chain while effectively funneling all monies to the aggregator who asks that you, pretty please, trust them that the penny you earned is proof that your song is being heard.

Also, many of these services remaster songs uploaded to them, then assign their ISRC to the new version and will only release that master. That means no money for you.

Only use these services to place one or two songs into the wild and solely for marketing purposes. Do not place your best songs there, either. Do not upload your entire album or catalog to them. You will be sorry when you try to monetize your music or promote yourself on YouTube.

DON'T BET YOUR BUSINESS
ON URBAN LEGENDS

There are rumors going around that PROs pay you $50 each time you perform live. This is NOT TRUE. Unless the gig is at a very large venue with massive ticket sales, reporting live performances at small-venue gigs will end up costing you more in time to fill out the paperwork and supply documentation than any royalties you earn from it. In other words: Not worth the time.

PERFORMING RIGHTS
ORGANIZATIONS & THE
PAYOUT INEQUALITY OF
THE BLANKET LICENSE

The only problem with blanket licenses is that the payout schedule will always be divvied up between the artists coming from The Majors and The Bigs.

If an DIY/Indie somehow manages to get massive airplay on terrestrial or other radio, the DIY/Indie will not get his share of the blanket license unless he specifically asks his PRO — and still only if the PRO says they can validate those numbers.

In any case, the DIY/Indie may have to wait a long time.

Sure, there are stories about quick payouts, but mostly those are urban legends, are the exception that proves the rule, or the artist knows somebody inside and well-placed.

SYNCH ROYALTIES & TV PRODUCERS REPORTING

Collection of synch royalties is completely dependent on producers of the television show sending cue sheets to the performing rights organizations so they can match their members or affiliates' songs to the final broadcasts. It is not unheard of for a production company to fail to send these in.

So publishers, music libraries, and catalog administrators must know which shows they signed agreements with, follow up with them, and build a fire under their backsides.

If the production company still does not supply the information, then the publishers, music libraries, and catalog administrators must contact the performing rights organizations associated with that song and give them the information.

The PROs will then attempt to confirm that report with the production company or a third party.

It has been suggested that YouTube should be considered a mass synchronization opportunity and, in fact, Google is now filing with the Copyright Office requests for permission to use music for streaming. They like to say they "cannot find" the owner to request permission from them.

Durden's Down & Dirty Hint & Tip

Sure, everybody wants to jump out of the gate with a massive sales or a kick-ass licensing deal with a multi-national company. But the truth is, those are made through relationships. *WHO DO YOU KNOW?*

PERFORMING RIGHTS ORGANIZATIONS & YOUR SONG INFORMATION

PROs are inundated with massive amounts of data, all coming piecemeal from hundreds of thousands of affiliates and members. The data might or might not be correct when it does get input. PROs in the U.S. all say they can not be held responsible for keeping accurate records once data is in their system EVEN IF INPUT CORRECTLY.

Budget cuts at the PROs have reduced staff and slowed implementation of technological solutions. Which means even though you may have all your information listed properly at your PRO, you may not have an ISWC assigned to your work for a long time.

Added to these challenges is the issue that each PRO has its own in-house technology, systems, and ways of collecting, paying, and so forth. <u>In other words, there is no industry standard for data collection, management, and inter-agency sharing in the music business.</u>

MUSIC LIBRARIES & RETITLING

Retitle. Remember that word and BEWARE of music libraries that retitle works they represent. When a library retitles your song and then places that song in a film, a TV broadcast, or other production that will be seen by the general public, unscrupulous libraries will say your song Title X has not been placed.

They can then keep all collected fees and you have no way of proving they owe you unless you happen to hear your song in a production.

DIGITAL DISTRIBUTORS
& REMASTERING

Please be advised as of this writing, I have not found one digital distributor / aggregator on this planet whose terms of service protect the income stream from a DIY/Indie's product.

In fact, most of the digital distributors / aggregators reserve the right to remaster your song/album, turning it into a completely new "version" that will then have assigned to it an ISRC associated with that company. That version will get played and sold, as well as licensed.

ALSO BEWARE the "publisher" who claims they will "get you on" all distribution channels in the world. For the most part these "publishers" are little more than sub-distributors using the likes of CD Baby, TuneCore, and other aggregators and digital distributors to get your product up and out into the wild.

Here's the problem with that: Your business deal is with the "publisher". Their business deal is with the aggregator or digital distributor. Therefore, if your "publisher" does not pay you, you will not be able to get your money from the digital distributor or aggregator because they will not recognize you as "on the deal".

This is not illegal, but it is scummy. This cheating has also happened with established artists. One established artist not only wrote all the songs, but paid all production costs, too, believing sales would then cover those costs and make a profit. Sales were phenomenal, but then no money came.

The artist thought her team was using a legitimate publisher. This "publisher" turned out to be a fly-by-night sub-distributor who took the money and ran.

KNOW WITH WHOM YOU DO BUSINESS.

Durden's Down & Dirty Look Inside the Performing Rights Organizations' Royalty Paying Methods

At music conferences, especially those specializing in Rap and Hip Hop, one would likely hear an expert on a panel: "You have to be ready for when it's your turn to 'be on.'"

Then another panelist, usually a rep from a PRO, would relate a story about the poor young fellow from the 'hood who wrote Hit X, and who then took his very first royalty check ever to the cash-checking store. But lo! When he arrived, he found the store wouldn't cash it because it was for five figures, and he couldn't convince them it wasn't a scam.

Then the young fellow would call his PRO rep for help and the rep would say, "Come to the office and we'll go set you up a bank account."

"It's my time to *be on*" became a rallying cry for those who thought they had the next big hit for the *rapper du jour* making it big on the airwaves. A once-and-done songwriting career? Really? That's all anybody could hope for?

The problem with such stories is that there can be no verification of them. Nobody wants to claim they made that money because all their relatives would come out of the woodwork asking for a share. I don't blame them for wanting to keep it to themselves. Still, it's hard to believe such massive payouts exist as a regular routine. There are several reasons for the doubt.

First, too many songwriters of verifiable hits, with split sheets in place, are still chasing their royalties years after the hit was played on radio or placed on an album.

Second, the massively convoluted royalty calculation methods employed by ASCAP, BMI, and SESAC. Their employees admit they can't figure it out. The PROs refuse to make their calculating and tracking methods transparent.

Things like that continue to help PROs lose prestige with their core constituents: Songwriters. Their reputations as protectors of songwriters have taken a well-deserved beating.

For instance, ASCAP's 20 pages of rules and policies attempt to explain their Survey and Distribution System. The opening statement in section 1.1 says "The ultimate purpose of the survey and distribution system is to ensure that royalty payments to members reflect fairly the value of performances in the various surveyed media, and that the methods and formulas employed for such distributions are disclosed fully and clearly to all members."

Sounds good, doesn't it? Let's get the next little tidbit in section 1.3: "...different types of performances have different values, even within the same medium....The weights assigned to performances are set forth in the Weighting Formula, which are applied equally to all works regardless of their identity."

Weighting Formula? Where is that? Let's turn eight pages to section 4. The Weighting Formula.

This formula recognizes over 10 categories of works that can qualify for royalties. If your song is to qualify as Theme, Background Music, Cue Music or Bridge Music, or announcement, then the piece must have:

4.3.1(i)(a) an accumulation of 40,000 radio and television Feature performance credits since October 1, 1959; *and*

4.3.1(i)(b) an accumulation of 10,000 radio and television Feature Performance credits during the five (5) latest available preceding fiscal survey years, toward which total not more than 3000 credits shall be counted for any one (1) of such survey years; provided, however, that when a work accumulates 300,000 radio and television Feature Performance credits it shall be deemed to be in compliance with this test.

IS YOUR HEAD SPINNING YET?

Of course your head is spinning. And that after only three paragraphs out of a 20-page policy guide.

I read just about the entire 20 pages of ASCAP's and the 10 pages of BMI's Royalty Policy Manual, and only skimmed SESAC's.

In any case, the upshot was this: They pay royalties to a highly select group. Can you guess who is in that group? Let's take a look at who comprises their governing boards:

ASCAP'S 24-member board has 12 writers and 12 publishers. Eight of the publishers are:
    •   Chairman and CEO of Sony/ATV Music Publishing.

- Chairman and CEO of the music publishing arm of Warner Music Group.
- U.S. President, Repertoire and Marketing, BMG.
- Past-president/CEO of Atlantic Records Nashville.
- Past-president, Marketing & Creative, BMG.
- Past-president/CEO of the U.S. division of the PolyGram International Publishing Group.
- Past-president of both MCA Music Publishing and Chrysalis Music Group, Inc.
- Past-president of EMI and Chappell/Intersong, among others.

Of BMI's 18-member board, all are associated with broadcasting and media conglomerates in radio and TV, and an investment group.

I found not one Independent, much less a DIY/Indie, represented anywhere.

So, what do you think? Do you think you can "trust" them to have your best interests at heart? I know what conclusion I've reached, and that is why I continue to say: Direct-to-fan, ladies and gentlemen.

Look, if a label comes looking for you, only then will you be in a position to negotiate a deal friendlier to you. Mind your business with an eye to serving your best interests. Devise a process to keep up with your product, sales outlets you use, and so forth. And, for goodness' sake, check your catalog listings on your PRO member portal regularly to see if they are staying accurate and have not let in any poachers.

Durden's Down & Dirty on Market Engagement

Can't sell downloads at a yard sale.
Challenges DIY/Indies face in the music industry

Ask anyone. They'll tell you it's a crazy-wild mess out there in the music industry. One way of summing up the conundrum: You can't sell downloads at a yard sale.

Consumers. Service providers and retailers for content providers. Licensees of content. I continue to talk to everyone wherever I meet them. One question they all get is this: What is your biggest challenge?

To consumers:
Getting the content when you want it.

To service providers:
Meeting the needs of content providers and licensees.

To online retailers/aggregators:
Selling/distributing content.

To content providers:
Making money with the original content you provide and protecting your intellectual property.

Consumers say streaming is expensive and aggravating —
free versions come with time commitments (ads) and lack of
choice. Many are weary of connecting new devices, learning
changing interfaces, fighting glitchy updated versions that
don't work, and not being able to access their purchased
music where and when they want it.

Listeners are often surprised to find the money they paid for
that one song they love is just a license to listen offline — but
only until they stop being a subscriber.

One-at-a-time downloads may build a massive library
consumers believe they own, but assembling playlists is
boring, inefficient, and doesn't well serve the artist or fan. As
one teenager overheard in a coffeeshop told a friend, "I'm
tired of downloading. Why can't I buy a whole bunch of
songs by one person so I can listen to them, like, back-to-back
or something? This is painful!"

Further harming artists is they can no longer engage with
fans. Why? Because of the new distribution system, artists
exist only behind a cyber wall built by digital aggregators.
The aggregator's customer is not the artist's customer.
Retaining the customer as theirs, aggregators do not share
deep sales data with the artists. In other words, artists can't
independently reach out a second time to their fans because
they don't know who they are.

True, the same challenge exists if product is sold in a brick-
and-mortar store. The difference is that online service
providers falsely market their package as a method to not
only find fans but stay in touch with them, too. This is simply
not how it works. How to overcome that?

This is where technology has become the DIY/Indie's friend. Just about every Web platform these days can handle direct sales. Online payment gateways like PayPal, Stripe, Square, and others are friendly to small business, protecting the financial privacy and safety of your customer with enterprise-level services at extremely affordable prices. These services do not hold your customer's data hostage: You get all the sales and contact information. Everybody wins.

The physical format is coming back strong. Vinyl albums (showing a 10-year growth pattern), CDs (never dead), and even cassette tapes are enjoying a resurgence. There are various drivers of this revival, but the main one is this: The retailer gets money upfront for the sale of a physical product that moves from one hand to another.

Those retailers are more often than not in the DIY/Indie world with independent record stores leading the charge, and DIY/Indie artists making sales at their shows — often autographed and personally handed to the fan. Nielsen said about the most current and complete annual numbers:

> In the physical realm, vinyl stayed strong, as sales of LPs hit a new record in 2015 — nearly 12 million units. This marks the 10th straight year of vinyl sales growth. The big winners in this realm were independent record stores, which drove 45% of all vinyl sales. The biggest genre for vinyl? Rock, with 68% of LP sales.

Notice the term is "sales", not units manufactured. Nielsen does not care how many units are manufactured. They only deal with final numbers of consumer interaction. Which, of course, brings up a huge point: How does Nielsen know what gets sold?

They only can report on sales that have gone through a third-party validation process with a service such as SoundScan or BuzzAngle, to mention two.

Artists planning tours, and in other ways marketing themselves, are interested in charting on Billboard or other genre-specific or regional music charts. All those charts require third-party validation of sales. One way to gauge success of a project, though not the only one, is charting. While the charting qualifying minimums used to be hundreds of thousands of radio spins and units sold, these days the minimums are oftentimes less than 5000.

IndieHitmaker.com is one company that does a very good job helping artists validate and report live show sales that count toward the charts. Bram Bessoff is the guy to see about this. We talk regularly.

But there's a bigger question you should ask yourself: Do you need to chart?

Sure, charting is great for the ego, especially if you rank high. But there is a huge group of DIY/Indie artists who, for whatever reason and it doesn't matter why not, are not interested in charting. These people are still selling a boatload of physical product at live shows and not reporting it to charting companies. As small businesses, they track sales for their own purposes, but they don't tell anybody about those numbers.

So, when we read the Nielsen report mentioned previously, we must realize there are a lot of other sales going on and there is no way to quantify how huge that market is.

What is clear is there's a much larger market for physical product sales and direct-to-fan engagement than what reaches the public in reports pushed out by the lazy media, which take their headlines directly from marketing agencies.

It is up to the artist to engage the fan.

It is up to the songwriter to engage the artist.

It is up to both artist and songwriter to protect and defend the very basis for their businesses: Intellectual property rights.

I know how difficult this can be. But, these actions can and must be systemized by making them a habitual part of the artist and songwriter's work flow. They cannot be automated as set-and-go like some service providers promise. Nor can they be ignored with a hope and prayer that somehow everything will turn out all right in the end as somebody else magically protects your property.

And, for all that is good and holy, these functions cannot be turned over willy-nilly to companies with business goals designed to take advantage of those with a loosey-goosey approach to protecting and defending their own business interests.

When Internet user numbers are deconstructed outside the influence of technology bubbles, investor pitch decks, industry-centric reports, and survey results extracted from baffling categories, one thing becomes clear:

> Most consumers have not wanted — and will never want — their music delivered as a rental. They want to own it, especially if they are spending money on the new delivery services that are limiting artist engagement and discovery.

In other words, these streaming services are saying that their portals are the best place to get discovered. But to understand the minuscule opportunity afforded new artists to be discovered, consider these numbers:

Thirty-six million people in the U.S. do not own a computer. That is, 11% of the U.S. population do not have a computer in their home. Most of those people do not access the Internet.

Worldwide Internet usage is 3.77 billion, or half of the world's population.

Spotify boasts that their worldwide user base is 40 million, making the company's global market share among Internet users around 1%.

Songs uploaded to the Internet from all sources are approaching 100 million, and that number grows by the tens of thousands every month.

Of those 40 million Spotify subscribers, the vast majority use the free version (which is ad-supported) and many of these same Spotify subscribers are also signed up to similar services such as SiriusXM, Pandora, etc.

These services also claim millions of users. Those millions for the most part are duplicated with Spotify. So, the user base — understand that to mean listeners — is reduced even further.

Yet to hear Spotify and Pandora and the others tell the story, you'd think the world was only listening to music through their services and that you, the new artist, will hit it big by putting your songs on their services — for per-song upload fees, of course.

Obviously, this is not how a successful career is built. The discovery of new talent by listeners is not enough to build a career on. A thriving career will never happen if one depends solely upon getting discovered on the Internet. Do not believe the urban legends pushed by digital distributors.

Throw in these services' lack of profit, minuscule paid-user bases, and overall user numbers artificially inflated by freemium versions (designed to influence investors to open their pocketbooks to bubble-sustaining levels), and you can see the music industry is not what The Bigs and The Majors want you to believe it is. Look, they have a service to sell. They will say whatever they must in order to get consumers to sign up. But what is good for a consumer is not good for you — the content creator, the artist, the I.P. owner.

In the meantime, notwithstanding the glowing giddy headlines, the bubble has burst for online retailers and those who aggregate that content for sale. Google Trends shows a five-year decline in searches for CD Baby, though searches for the second-place company, TuneCore, remained steady during the same period.

Interesting note: After a decline of some years, during this same five-year period, copyright infringement topic searches again rose, matching or eclipsing the search counts for the two popular aggregators.

This tells us that content providers — songwriters and artists — have gotten more savvy.

Online distributors' glory days are over. Frankly, those glory days only existed in paid-for editorial content, as urban legends pushed by experts hiding as silent stakeholders, or in fairytales sermonized by clueless fawning media hacks who will print anything given to them. The cult of personality comes with a dollar sign, too: Think about the mess that is called Tidal.

Google Trends shows searches for information on streaming surpass searches for digital downloads and sales of physical product. This begs two questions:

- Who is making the money, and on whose backs is it being made?
- Do search trends prove streaming is a viable business model to be embraced by DIY/Indies?

Entertainment attorneys share war stories with me — with zero client-identifying information, of course — about problems with collecting monies rightfully due their clients. Big obstructions to hard-earned paydays include:

- Lack of or incomplete documentation of ownership stakes;
- Missing or incomplete metadata;

- Missing (or never created) split sheets and other ownership registration and verification with a third-party validator;
- Placing a song or an entire album with fly-by-night sub-distributors;
- Placing entire catalogs with distributors and sub-distributors who promise to get songs out worldwide — as if that is the main path to sales success;
- Digital aggregators claiming co-publishing status with their customers, and making those claims inside the performing rights organizations' member portals.

We round out our understanding by digging into news articles and press releases about the assaults on intellectual property rights. From these we can reach certain conclusions that will allow us to make better decisions about who gets to represent our music online.

There's a great need to understand the challenges and dynamics of the music business as they apply to songwriters, or as they are otherwise known: The largest unprotected contributors to music I.P. in the world.

While not all independent songwriters are also the artist, many are. Decisions made based on experts' out-of-date advice adversely affects all DIY/Indies' income streams. Those income streams include:

- Writing:
    - > Lyrics.
    - > Music.
- Publishing:
    - > Licensing display of lyrics and inclusion of music: TV, movies, ad campaigns, gaming, masters, stems and pieces, covers, etc.
    - > Display rights (lyrics on services such as Shazzam, SoundHound, and Gracenote), and print rights (sheet music).
- Retail sales:
    - > Online.
    - > Offline: Brick-and-mortar, at live shows.
- Interactive and non-interactive Internet radio/streaming:
    - > YouTube song video plays.
    - > Fan covers of song paired with video on YouTube.
    - > Spotify- and Pandora-types of streaming services.
    - > Other non-interactive Internet radio usages.
    - > Terrestrial radio.
- Placements with other artists' projects:
    - > Deals with First-Run Rights intact.
    - > Mechanicals.

How do you have a chance to prove you have a right to any of the above income streams? Paperwork.

Nobody likes paperwork. Many are hesitant or too lazy to take the required time — even if that time will protect them and their property.

Lack of this proof benefits digital aggregators and the PROs: They owe you nothing if they cannot find you or if you cannot prove you own the songs. The vast majority of (if not all) digital aggregators and digital distributors are the enemy of content creators and owners.

Further, these services' terms of service cheat songwriters, artists, and publishers. Certain of these services regularly remaster artist-uploaded content and assign their branded International Standard Recording Code number (ISRC). They also assign the same ISRC to multiple unrelated songs, making a muddy mess of who gets royalties for which song.

These distributors also leave it to artists to examine, investigate, and chase their sub-distributors or upline retail chain while telling the artist they have no choice who the distributor does business with. Their contracts say if you don't get all money due you, don't complain to them. As an example of widespread industry practice, CD Baby's contract* states:

> CD Baby shall have no liability to you for failure to audit or investigate any accountings rendered to it by any Licensees.

and

> You shall remain solely responsible for enforcing the removal of Your Content from our Licensees' websites and services in the event such Licensees fail to remove Your Content following receipt of a Takedown Notice or following the termination of

---

* This language is taken verbatim from CD Baby's online contract that must be agreed to before you can use their service.

any rights granted to such Licensees by CD Baby; provided, however, that CD Baby may, in its sole and absolute discretion, continue to assist you to effectuate the removal of Your Content from Licensees' websites and services. CD Baby may, but need not, provide you with notice in the event CD Baby terminates or allows to expire any authorizations previously granted to a Licensee for the distribution of Your Content.

and

The parties hereto agree and acknowledge that the relationship between them is that of independent contractors.**

and

CD Baby may assign its rights and obligations under this Agreement at any time to any party. You may not assign your rights and/or obligations under this Agreement without obtaining CD Baby's prior written consent.

These contracts are so one-sided as to be laughable. The rot goes deep, it is across the board, and there is no cure within the system.

By putting their own identification on new master recordings, digital aggregators have been successful in having rightful I.P. owners' music videos taken down off YouTube, Vimeo, etc. for copyright infringement. The artist then must produce a mountain of documentation as proof they have the right to use their own song.

** *Independent contractor status would be fine except that CD Baby is listing themselves as co-publisher — which means co-owner — with a 50% share of songs they register on your behalf with the PROs, which takes them out of independent contractor status and into business partner status, thus breaking their own contract with their customers.*

YouTube is not happy about this situation and has begun to put other measures in place to protect the rightful owner, pushing the money toward the artist or other lawful holders of rights. They are being fought in the press and in the boardrooms. This is why since 2016 you have been seeing such negative and vitriolic press against YouTube from, for instance, Irving Azoff, attorney to the mega-stars.

In the first part of 2016, Mr. Azoff became quite vocal about YouTube, railing about how Google was using the Digital Millennium Copyright Act to cheat artists. The DMCA is an 18-page, government-mandated law involving a process to protect I.P. rights. Because of the fast-changing nature of technology, the DMCA was out of date the day it was signed.

However, like all online companies must, YouTube also had no choice but to comply with the DMCA. Millions of companies, not just YouTube, are attempting to do it. However, Mr. Azoff all but said YouTube was the author of the DMCA for its own evil means.

Understanding that YouTube was implementing protections for content creators, I publicly proclaimed Mr. Azoff's righteous indignation did not pass my BS meter. Not long after calling him out, I found Mr. Azoff was entering a new pony in the royalty-collecting race. Yes, Mr. Azoff was setting up a new performing rights organization. He thought putting pressure on services would allow him to negotiate and collect a higher rate than the Royalty Rate Board allowed.

I read everything I could get my hands on about how he was planning on becoming a de facto performing rights organization, and my respect for Mr. Azoff plummeted. Was he attempting to line his pockets by using as pawns content creators and their ability to monetize their privately owned content?

Who can depend upon an expert's recommendation if said expert does not disclose that they work for or have a backdoor investment in the solution provider they endorse?

In other words: Where's the full disclosure?

Full disclosure is especially important if an expert holds himself out to be an independent source of real information upon which to build a solid career.

Of course, as a born sceptic always willing to dig to the foundation of a situation, my research shows that many experts on the music industry have deep and abiding connections — sometimes financial — to the major players.

Having taken an early retirement or been downsized when their company was rolled up into one of The Bigs, these former employees become consultants. The problem with their advice is that, while it is said to help the DIY/Indie, it actually serves The Bigs, The Majors, and Tech Giants' businesses first and foremost.

Instead, by following that advice the DIY/Indie is harmed, often irreparably. The Majors don't care about that because their main goal is to protect their market share. Some of their financial guns are aimed straight at getting rid of the competition. If they can do that by feeding hungry, lazy mouthpieces the party line, they'll do it.

Do not misunderstand me: This is the free market — capitalism — in all its glory. I am not saying competition should not exist. I am not asking for a level playing field because socialism never works.

I am pointing out that The Majors' sharp business practices have, in point of fact, destroyed any hope for the music industry to thrive. The Bigs have cut off their noses to spite their faces. These practices are not new but have reached critical mass.

Peter Frampton's second album sold 300,000 copies. These days that would be a massive hit. But back in 1975, it was considered a failure by the industry because sales did not meet or beat his first album, *Frampton Comes Alive!*, which was the breakout album for him, going platinum eight times. One million units of the double album sold in one week. You'd think that would be great money for Frampton, but the resulting comedy of errors hurt his career for years.

Multiply knee-jerk rationales and short-term thinking many times over, and you see a badly run industry that destroyed Peter's — and many others' — earning potential.

To protect my customers, collaborators, or readers, I never point them in a distribution or sales direction where their I.P. will be under attack, tracked loosely, or where they could lose control of it. To protect myself in my songwriting business, my collaborator — also known as my business partner — must agree to strong process controls when it comes to documenting, validating, and monetizing our mutual intellectual property.

As stated earlier, the bubbles have burst on digital music providers, many of which are publicly traded. Their reported fast growth numbers, artificially inflated through industry consolidations and other buyouts, have left many over-leveraged, with no more investors on the horizon, and desperate to satisfy stockholders.

I've communicated with a few far-sighted individuals around the world who see this demise clearly and are attempting to implement Blockchain technology in various permutations for collaborating, catalog documentation, information sharing, and direct-to-fan sales that cut out all or most middlemen and The Bigs, The Majors, and certain Tech Giants.

Blockchain was touted for a while, but it appears to be a non-starter for the DIY/Indie at this time. In February of 2017, a press release said the dotBlockchain Music Project (dotBC) is now being financially backed by Canadian music rights organization SOCAN, its wholly owned subsidiary MediaNet, Songtrust, CD Baby, and FUGA (a digital distributor/aggregator). The partners announced they will contribute vital technical and financial resources to the project, which will allow dotBC to accelerate its product development efforts.

Let me prophesy here just a bit: The power of Blockchain will become laser-focused on The Bigs and The Majors, and the cost to deploy for DIY/Indies will become prohibitive, thereby cutting them out again.

The performing rights organizations (ASCAP, BMI, SESAC) continue to lose prestige. Their reputations as protectors of songwriters have taken a well-deserved beating. Entering the music industry with levels of savvy higher than new entrants from the past, independent songwriters/publishers are more aware than ever of the dismal success rate of PROs on behalf of songwriters. The Majors and The Bigs can no longer hide their self-serving intentions because of a pesky group: The DIY/Indies who are comfortable doing some research.

PROs know certain digital aggregators/distributors are taking half of publishing rights from publishers (including songwriters who act as their own publisher) once masters are uploaded to those services.

The PROs address this issue by saying digital aggregators' terms of service allow it. Those are misleading statements at best, flat-out lies at worst. If the statements are incorrect, then does that mean our performing rights organizations are clueless? However, if they have a clue, then are they liars concerning this matter? Or, hmmm…do we have collusion among these entities against content creators?

Music business schools often get financial support from the entrenched ruling industry; often their department heads are former industry elites. While some individuals at these schools love the book I wrote — *Navigating the New Music Business as a DIY & Indie* — and want me to come teach workshops that will benefit their students, when they try to get permission for even a one-off event, the answer from on high is always No.

Yet, these same schools fall prey to the cult of personality and favor panels stacked with big names teaching information that is erroneous. The rooms may be packed, but the information dispensed is harmful. Many a small music business owner, with hopes of growing large enough to support their family for years to come, has simply been destroyed because of decisions made based on harmful information.

Thank goodness, though, the messaging is getting out. During one of these university events a client of mine attended, he was appalled at how uninformed the panel members were. He texted me a list of the panel members, some of whom I know, and some of the wrong information they were still preaching even after I had sat down with them and explained multiple times why they were not making money anymore.

As one man said in a Facebook conversation: "The record companies ended themselves. They made all the money. And the artist — unless they sold millions of records — had no leverage." Then again, Peter Frampton, among others, sold millions and where was their leverage?

Frustrated with that market dynamic, songwriters/artists opted out and went their own independent way. That's what gave rise to CD Baby in its first incarnation: Artist-friendly and affordable small-batch product production for sale at live shows.

It was a hit. I loved the company — back then. Then came the international conglomerates. They pretty much succeeded in killing what was left of the music business by jumping over dollars to save a few pennies. There are now no promotion, distribution, or publicity people at the labels ready to help the artists. In effect, The Majors and The Bigs killed each other.

Here is what one frustrated man, who is still performing after a 30+ year career, wrote to me:

> Even the Indie labels aren't independent anymore. The last large indie was A&M and even they sold out to the corporations before it was over. BTW, no matter what you see, there are only two major labels left: Universal and Sony. They absorbed all the labels. The Internet has never, and I don't think will ever, break a major record. This is how it will be until someone completely rebuilds the industry.
>
> I was on the A&M label roster in the 1980s. Then I had a Sony distribution deal in Europe for many years with different labels. But not anymore. It's the same now with artists everywhere. They have no industry to really be a part of. Also, in this day and age of "instant" success, no one hones their craft anymore. There was a time you were on the road, in the clubs working on your songs and show for 6-10 years so that when you got signed you were ready to become that "overnight" sensation that you were called. Nowadays, most young people don't have that kind of patience to do that.

But why? Because instant fame followed by instant money is promised by shysters, and too many artists believe it is that easy: Record. Release. Reap!

It is important to note here that those who perform covers do not have the same business challenges or goals as those who create content, and this book is aimed at those who create content. If you create content, then you should be making money on several fronts.

Many are saying the Internet is re-creating the era of the small venue.

Bands performing their original material are connected with fans via social media platforms which can be clunky — even punishing users by using ever-changing algorithms. But bands and solo or duo artists can book shows using DIY groups and Internet fan-marketing and venue-booking tools. Add to that selling merch at their shows such as t-shirts, stickers, vinyl, CDs, tapes, books, etc. and the profits can go higher.

Connecting to fans is hard work. The ego takes a beating. That's why it is easier for an artist to exist behind a wall built by digital aggregators. But the aggregators consider your customer to be their customer and will not share buyers' contact information.

In radio, if they can't pigeonhole your music into one of about five formats, you don't get played. CD Baby says it has 850 genres. How does that even work? Try finding an artist without knowing their name. Where do you begin searching? Consequently, new artists get cheated if they try to get noticed or earn royalties through the online streaming portals. They are done in by devious user agreements, fluctuating service provider interfaces, updated interface versions that don't work, and listeners not easily having their purchased music where and when they want it.

The crucial piece missing in today's music business environment is the ability to be discovered. The live performance circuit, once robust, nearly died. It is showing signs of life, faint though they be. As Bram Bessoff said, "Artists need to rethink their direct-to-fan engagement strategy."

Do you have a
direct-to-fan engagement strategy?

Do you own your sales pipeline?

Can you get hold of your fans without
Tech Giants controlling the process?

KEN BONFIELD SAYS:
Before you decide a song
or album hasn't worked,
wait a minimum of one
year. Yes, it takes at
least that long to get
through the distribution
system and onto a
playlist. However, that
doesn't mean it cannot
be earning. You can see
retail sales of CDs,
downloads, and albums
long before streaming
royalties kick in.

What makes a one-hit wonder?

Lack of a team with good paperwork and well-defined roles contributing to the final product, tour, and more. It sounds almost clichéd, but nobody has the time to wear all hats required to run a music business, be the creative force behind it, and be the front man.

Now comes the challenge, wouldn't you agree? Yes, the challenge of affording a TEAM. I've talked to a lot of artists who ask for recommendations for managers and such. I ask them about their tour schedule, and merch and album sales.

They say — and I'm not kidding you — they *always* say they are looking for others to work "for a piece of the action", a percentage of the profits *the manager will generate* on behalf of the artist, yet the artist has never sold a single song, much less a ticket to a show featuring them.

It amazes me that others are asked to work for free to promote — heck, build! — an artist's career. So, if managers can't, won't, and don't work for free, how does an artist get to where they can afford label and management services to get their business to another level?

There are several things they can do. They can go to family and friends for funding. They can do an Indiegogo-type of campaign to raise funds. Though if nobody knows who they are, obviously funds won't accrue as fast. Lots of folks will not lend money to relatives just because they can play the guitar or write a song.

The person who wants to be in the business has the responsibility to test the waters first.

- Can they attract even a local following of people who will come to more than just one show?
- Does any audience member want to buy a t-shirt or CD?
- Can they sell a ticket to a show?

In other words, does anybody care about your music enough to spend money on you? Often the answer is no. Why is that? The top reasons are:

1. Boring show.
2. Boring show.
3. And boring show.

There is a huge lack of showmanship.

There's a myth going around that says it is the audience's responsibility to connect to the music. So, on the stage you've got an artist that writes songs about *their life, their experiences*. If that life or experience or story or whatever it is they are singing about resonates with the audience, then that's a good thing. A regularly occurring problem is that usually the singer is doing a very bad job of presenting that song live.

Why would an audience leave work, go home, bathe, change their clothes, drive to a venue, pay for parking and dinner and oftentimes a babysitter *and* drinks *and* gas for the car, *and* then sit there *and* pay for the privilege of hearing exactly what they hear on a recorded version?

Or worse yet, a bad version of the recording? One where the artist rushes through their set, doesn't let the audience applaud, won't look or smile at or thank the audience, and mumbles between songs? It happens all the time.

Thus, some of the growing malaise of potential music fans can be laid at the artists' feet. The artist has to give some thought to live shows as seen through the eyes of the audience. The show is not about the artist, it's about surprising the audience with art shared with them and seen live in front of them.

Once an artist can prove they have even a small following, they can then go to friends and family and ask for investment money. Maybe an Indiegogo campaign might benefit them.

If they keep doing that, then a strong Indie label might want to give them a look.

- Are you a carbon copy of everybody else out there? Imitation may be the sincerest form of flattery, but whose tickets, albums, and merch are you trying to sell?
- When the audience leaves, do they say *well, ho hum, they did alright, but I know others who did the **covers** better*?
- Or, do you have a style all your own? And by style, I mean clothes and attitude, too.
- Are you genuine with the audience? Do they see the real you?
- Are you giving *to* them or expecting *from* them?

You aren't crazy.

If you feel like you are going crazy in the music business, you aren't alone. It seems that, even though we do as we are told to be successful, things don't happen as they should.

We aren't crazy.

The industry really is that messed up.

Since the 1930s to 1950s until around 10-15 years ago, those in the business could confidently rely on income from sales of physical product. The first big change hit the industry when massive public adoption of in-home listening of music on a turntable or radio made sheet music almost obsolete overnight. Napster was the first pebble to start the current avalanche that buried income streams from physical product. People started expecting to get music at no cost to themselves. And they were downloading and copying and sharing digital copies.

It became easy — and cheap — to get music.

Record stores went out of business. Whole chains disappeared. Major labels have been downsizing for years. What do you need a sales force for if you've got no product, right?

And then…

…gone with it was the dependable income stream for the major labels and their publishing companies. Then the downturn in the economy – twice since 2000 – from which we've not yet recovered, so people spend less.

Then came the massive consolidations which were nothing more than a stopgap strategy to stop the bleeding. It's hurting the promotion and accounting staff, and the top execs, too. So, what we had was the perfect storm of less disposable income and a technology revolution making music so available that it was no longer a prized commodity.

What did all that mean for songwriters and artists?

It meant that all music was available everywhere all the time. Regular fans ceased to be excited anymore.

Therefore, "Bleh, I'll get it later, *maybe*" became the norm for how music was consumed. Bored fans led to no sales, which meant empty pockets.

To avoid falling into a creative rut, artists often turned to songwriters looking to place music. That was a very good financial strategy for both songwriter and artist, by the way. However, there is a simple thing contributing to the massive reduction of songwriters pitching artists or artists recording a song they didn't write: Paperwork. Nobody wants to do it.

Creatives need lots of mental excitement and stimuli. That's the nature of creatives and will never change. Paperwork is the opposite of exciting and most ignore it until finally it bites them in the butt. So shared marketing leading to profits is almost extinct.

There was a time in Nashville when thousands of songs each year were placed by songwriters with artists. That number is now in low hundreds. Publicly you won't hear Nashville admit it, but hang around enough and you will hear producers bemoan their downsizing as they move their studios from swanky digs to home basements.

Yet artists need other songwriters to bring *that something new* to their table. It makes perfect sense when you think about it. Everybody has a sweet talent lane they shine in. But when the audience begins not to be able to tell the difference between an artist's new and old songs, then fans are lost. It is the rare person who likes the exact same meal day in and day out. It is the same with fans.

SURVIVAL

REGISTRATIONS TO PROTECT I.P.

FINAL MASTERS:
Performing Rights Organizations
Copyright.gov

SONGWRITERS:
Performing Rights Organizations

PUBLISHERS:
Performing Rights Organizations

LABELS:
SoundExchange.com

ARTISTS:
SoundExchange.com

Do not confuse registrations above with signing up for services from any company that supplies distribution, or one that says they will get your information to any of the agencies above, because they do not. They keep your information in their own proprietary database.

A Short History of the Modern Music Business

Pre-1920s: Touring vaudeville troupes.

1920s to 1970s:
Radio, touring performers, phonographic disc records, vinyl records.

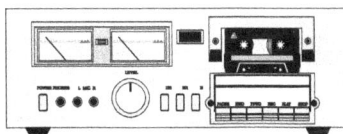

1960s to late 1980s:
Radio, touring performers, vinyl records, various tape formats.

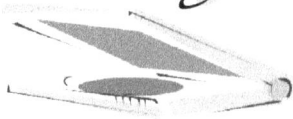

Late 1980s to 1998:
Radio, touring performers, the push to sell product by converting to CDs.

1998 to 2015:
Radio, touring performers, the push of streaming services.

Technology changes kill one format and bring another to life. Never depend on technology to be constant.

2016 until who knows when: Radio (with diminished popularity), resurgence of touring performers, falling off of paid streaming services, resurgence of physical formats.

The only constants?
Change and *TALENT!*

Tony Wasilewski

Label Founder and Producer

Hot Shoe Records, Inc., Atlanta, Georgia

HotShoeRecords.com

Year Founded: 2005

Albums Released: 14

Mission Statement:
To document who we will
want to remember in the Jazz world.

CATEGORY: MARKET RESEARCH
Get ready for surprises.

Q: What was the biggest surprise you experienced after setting up your label?

TONY: The biggest surprise was the *hyped* promise of the Internet. In the early days of the Internet, the promise was that all anybody had to do was put something on the Net and — bam! — somehow everybody would know about it. That was *definitely* not true.

Q: Which meant…

TONY: I had to rethink what my marketing would look like. Internet presence is important, but it is just table stakes.

Q: What did that rethink lead to?

TONY: I began looking at publications that featured the genre I was producing, which is Jazz. I had money to give them for ad space. They had space to sell. You would think this was a perfect fit. But they didn't want my money.

Q: What? Why?

TONY: Because they never heard of my label or the few artists I recorded up to that point. I also think that financially things were better for the publications at that time — they had not yet felt the pinch of advertising money migrating to the Internet. They said *no, thank you.*

Q: What was your next big surprise?

TONY: How much competition there was. I did not think there was a lot of *independent* Jazz being made. Boy, was I wrong. Hot Shoe Records released its first album through CD Baby in 2006. That same week, on CD Baby alone, 32 other Jazz albums were released. Basically, all of these were also from independent labels or artist self-releases. I knew I would be up against established labels like Concord, Blue Note, ECM, etc. But I didn't expect so much activity from smaller entities.

Q: Sounds like you've had many opportunities to pivot.

TONY: You could say that, yes. Plus, I must know who my competition is. Where are they selling? Is it working? What are their strengths? What are my weaknesses? Stuff like that. In corporate-speak, you would say SWOT analysis has to be done. Strengths, weaknesses, opportunities, and threats both of my competition and for Hot Shoe Records. Add in all the

DIY/Indies whose sales or markets I will never be able to track or identify, then you can see marketing is not as easy as it sounds.

CATEGORY: BUSINESS STRUCTURE

Q: Let's talk a bit about how you structured your company. Are you an LLC, incorporated, or…?

TONY: Hot Shoe Records is organized as an LLC.

Q: Why did you choose this business structure?

Tony: An LLC provides some basic protection for personal assets and allows for relatively simpler handling of federal and state taxes.

Q: From the description of how you run your business — the details we will get into later — it seems that your label is mission-based. Can you tell us more about that?

TONY: Yes, I can. I happen to love Jazz. When I moved to Atlanta, of course I looked into the Jazz scene. I was amazed at the talent here that seemed to be flying under the radar and just subsisting.

So, I thought that one thing I might be able to do about that would be to record the best artists and distribute their work to a larger audience. I saw an opportunity to make a business based around my passion by giving new talent a high-quality opportunity to successfully get recognition and compensation for their creativity and art and maybe help enable Jazz to be the career of their choice.

Atlanta was already established as a Rap and Hip Hop center and if it was to be known for Jazz, a chronicle of what was happening would be needed in a form that could be widely distributed.

Q: Tell us a little bit about that passion. Obviously, you want to help do…what?

TONY: As has often been pointed out, Jazz is America's only original art form. Jazz exists because of a quintessential American characteristic: We are the melting pot. When an African sense of rhythm was combined with a European sense of melody, a new music emerged which allowed its practitioners to express their own emotions, aspirations, and accomplishments.

And that music, Jazz, has been evolving with the human spirit ever since.

For example, somebody playing the Blues or Ragtime said, "You know, I'm going to do something different with this tune." Next thing you know, experimentation and improvisation became the things to do.

We went from Ragtime to New Orleans Jazz to Big Band to Swing to Be-Bop to Post-Bop/Cool to Soul Jazz to Modern to Post-Modern to Fusion…And it has been embraced worldwide with especially notable contributions, for example, from Brazil and Cuba.

Luckily, along the way somebody got the idea to record some of that experimentation; and aren't we glad they did? We've got recordings of Bechet, Bix, Kid Ory, Nick Larocca, Goodman, Miles, Monk, Chet Baker, Coltrane, and many others. All as they invented and reinvented the art form.

I set my label up to encourage that experimentation and invention while documenting those I believe will make a long-lasting contribution to the art form and who may be of historical significance.

Q: Give us an example of that experimentation.

TONY: A prime example is Russell Gunn. Hot Shoe Records did an entire album of Russell and Elektrik Butterfly weaving together elements of Heavy Metal and Hip Hop into a Progressive Jazz style, while covering eight Black Sabbath tunes. Another example is the French band DJAZIL, in which a steel pan drum set is the lead singer.

Q: Have you ever been tempted to stray from your core mission? If yes, why? If no, why not? And how has that turned out?

TONY: No. Focus is critical if resources are to be utilized in an optimum manner.

Q: Final comments on this section?

TONY: Jazz as an art form will remain, but within the structure of that art form, where will the next evolution come from? What will it look like? Jazz is a language, not just a musical form. Fluency in that language allows practitioners to interact with each other very freely and that leads to innovation. We should be excited about this, not scared…and be ready to document where it leads to.

CATEGORY: DISTRIBUTION

Q: Let's talk distribution. What percentage of your releases are through physical distribution and what are through digital?

TONY: During most of the existence of Hot Shoe Records, in the recording industry as a whole, CDs have outsold digital distribution by dollar volume. Recently, digital has become more important, but I think Jazz lovers (more than many other music lovers) also appreciate the package that the music is delivered in and the information that comes with it. For Hot Shoe Records, CD distribution still dominates.

Q: Physical distribution. That includes...

TONY: Sales at live shows are very important, especially within a year of the release of an album. Online sales through third-party sites and through the Hot Shoe Records website also contribute significantly.

Q: Digital distribution. Does this include single-song releases and albums or just albums?

TONY: The right approach includes a combination of whole album and single-song sales. Single song allows price-sensitive listeners to purchase what they consider to be the highlight tracks of the album. It is important to note, however, that Jazz albums tend to be thematic and need to be listened to as a whole. A good example on Hot Shoe Records is *Imagine Nation* by Darren English. Three of the tracks comprise a suite written for Nelson Mandela. Not listening to all three tracks would muddle the artistic message at the very least. Also, *Jazz Contrasted* by Joe Gransden and Russell Gunn is a tribute to trumpeter Kenny Dorham with tracks selected to show the many sides of this underappreciated artist.

Q: Who do you use for digital distribution?

TONY: CD Baby. They do an efficient job of getting product into a myriad of online retail stores and streaming services. However, once my back catalog gets large enough, I should be able to represent my label to these retail stores. But that's in the future.

Q: Other than the digital distribution services from CD Baby, does the company perform any other services for you? If yes, what are they and what is your opinion of those? Does CD Baby also offer your albums in physical format? Do they fulfill?

TONY: Yes, they do physical sales fulfillment by shipping CDs from the inventory we provide to them. They take a fee for this service, which is subtracted from the album sale price, but it is fairly reasonable, so it still makes sense to be onboard with them for physical distribution.

Q: Why do you choose to sell from both your website and other sites?

TONY: Sometimes buyers are skittish when purchasing from a site they do not know. We give them options instead of losing the sale. Also, when a purchase is made on our website, there is no sales fee deducted as there is on CD Baby or other third-party sites.

Q: You have U.S. distribution. What about internationally?

TONY: Hot Shoe Records has a distribution relationship with a company specializing in the Japanese market. CDs are preferred in Japan and they love Jazz, so this represents a great opportunity.

Q: You once used Amazon for music sales. Why stop?

TONY: Wasn't profitable. Having Amazon do fulfillment is expensive and it was another lesson that mere presence on the Internet (even on the top online retailer) is no guarantee of sales. Also, Amazon's sales reporting tools were difficult to use.

CATEGORY: CHOOSING ARTISTS

Q: How do you go about choosing artists to record and release?

TONY: I look for five things. **One:** Artistry. Does what they do allow me to differentiate them in the marketplace or do they sound like everybody else? **Two:** Does the artist have conceptual imagination we can build on? **Three:** Does the artist have technical ability, *chops* as it is often called? **Four:** Are they new or evolving? **Five:** Do they have stage presence, and can they connect with the audience?

Q: Let's take the first one: Does what they do allow you to differentiate them in the marketplace or do they sound like everybody else? Explain why this is important to your label.

TONY: My job as the label is to sell. If I cannot tell the difference between what an artist is doing and what others are doing, then that makes my job of selling much harder.

Q: Because...

TONY: Because I have nothing to point to that is different. I would be lying if I said, "Try this artist. They are different from or better than what you've heard." Budgets are tight, and don't think they aren't. I don't have time or money to waste.

Q: Two: Does the artist have conceptual imagination you can build on?

TONY: Yes. I highly encourage a mix of originals and covers on an album. But I want the artist to be able to say, "I hear it this way." Then they must be able to bring that concept to life and carry it through the album. We want unique and challenging arrangements that audiences will want to hear.

Q: Three: Does the artist have technical ability, *chops* as it is often called? Can they do it once, and then can they do it again?

TONY: Exactly. Several things go into this. Recording is one thing, but most artists will make a good portion of their income from live performance. What can be done once in-studio might be groundbreaking and awesome, but if they cannot do it live repeatedly? That's not good in Jazz. Live Jazz should be just as good or better than the recording.

Also, for new artists, I encourage them to bring in a singer on a song or two. This proves they can work with a singer, which is important because most Jazz artists need to know how to "comp" other artists and not just dominate the conversation. If they can "comp" a singer well, they can probably "comp" anyone.

Q: In other genres, such as Rock or Pop or Hip Hop, it is almost an expected joke that the stage performance will never be as good as the recorded version. Does this hold true for Jazz?

TONY: Hopefully not! Even starting with the same arrangement, a Live Jazz performance should highlight the spontaneous interplay between the musicians and showcase the solo ability of the artists as much or more than the original recording.

Q: Four: Are they new/evolving?

TONY: This goes to the core mission of my label. If they have previously released recorded music, their contributions have been already at least partly documented. Thus, since resources are limited, they must be applied to expand the slate of artists as much as possible. However, great artists develop and evolve over time. Perhaps it appears as new tonality or phrasings that they haven't used before. Or maybe a horn player hones a decent singing voice over the years. Such changes/advancements need to be chronicled as well.

Q: Five: Do they have stage presence, and can they connect with the audience?

TONY: While Jazz is an inherently expressive musical form, an audience still wants to connect with the artist on a person-to-person level. This does not come naturally to many people even in everyday interactions. So, add the pressure of the stage and performance and you can see how it would be more difficult to do. However, this connection is important because live performances are a major source of sales and achieving rapport with fans is crucial for the career of most musicians.

CATEGORY: THE NATURE OF THE DEAL

Q: How do you go about signing an artist?

TONY: Technically, I don't sign them. Traditionally, a label would sign an artist to X amount of years and two, three, or more albums. Often labels would front the money for tours, recording, production, marketing, etc. Artists might get an advance, but this was little more than a loan that would have to be paid back. And artists would only get paid after all label expenses were recouped.

Q: But Hot Shoe Records doesn't do that?

TONY: No. We have what we call a Development Investment Agreement. Basically, it looks like the following. We never ask the artist for money. We don't give advances or do signing bonuses. We pay all recording and production expenses, including any side musicians we hire. Sidemen get paid upfront, plus they get copies of the album they can use for self-promotion. We make sure everybody is rehearsed well. We have paid the delivery and setup costs for specific pianos when a guest artist is an endorsed artist of a particular brand. We schedule all recording time and generally manage the project.

Q: In other words, Hot Shoe Records acts as the Executive Producer.

TONY: Executive Producer and Producer. Besides providing funding and logistics, we try to make sure the project will have reasonable commercial prospects by helping to define the musical plan with the artist. The Producer must be an advocate for both the artist and the audience, and achieving the proper balance while still fully supporting the artist's vision is one of the greatest challenges and rewards of the process. Hot Shoe Records participates in the studio and equipment selection and in "getting sound" for the project. It also is intimately involved in the mixing of each album, usually in consultation with the artist.

Q: Liner notes include everybody that is involved in the project?

TONY: Absolutely yes. Besides obviously giving credit to all musicians on the recording, all primary audio engineers, producers, graphic artists, writers, photographers, conductors, composers, and song copyright owners are listed.

Q: But how does the artist make money?

TONY: In a few ways. One: Because our featured artists do not have to pay us back for the costs to produce, record, and market their album, they are already well ahead of the game. They get a high-quality product and it doesn't cost them anything but a commitment to the project, undivided attention to their craft, and their time.

Two: They get promotional copies they can use for self-promotion to venues, magazines, or however they want to use them.

Three: Once sales commence, they immediately get a percentage of the sales. Hot Shoe Records does not require the recouping of all project expenses before paying out to the artist.

Four: If the artist composes original tunes for an album, the ownership of the composition remains with the artist, who can market it through selling sheet music or in other ways.

Q: What happens if pressing needs to go into a second or third run?

TONY: The development agreement typically calls for this to occur on a cost-sharing basis between the artist and Hot Shoe Records. However, the agreement also allows for the label to put up all the money required and then to recoup the artist's share of the pressing costs via future sales.

CATEGORY: PROTECTING INTELLECTUAL PROPERTY

Q: Do you have a publishing company?

TONY: No. As mentioned previously, Hot Shoe Records allows composition copyright to remain with the artist.

Q: For covers recorded under your label, how do you confirm rights are properly paid for?

TONY: Fortunately, it is fairly straightforward to do. For covers, the Harry Fox Agency is always the first stop. For most songs they handle 100% of the copyright licensing. When Harry Fox does not handle all licensing for a given song, we contact the remaining owner(s) directly. This requires more work, but it doesn't happen all that frequently. As part of the development agreement, if the artist contributes original compositions to a recording, the artist grants a license to Hot Shoe Records for the use of the song(s) on that album.

Q: For original songs by your artists, how do you help them document their ownership stake? Do you help them with split sheets (in the case of the artist recording a song written by themselves and another)?

TONY: Hot Shoe Records encourages artists to establish their own publishing company (or join one) if they are not already affiliated with one. And, of course, they are listed as composer in the album notes.

Q: Who makes sure the artist (as writer and/or publisher of their original works) lists their releases with their performing rights organization?

TONY: Hot Shoe Records always encourages newer artists to form (best option) or join a publishing company and has guided them to the major performing rights organizations (U.S. PROs: ASCAP, BMI, SESAC) to register their compositions with them. Established artists usually already have their own publishing companies and register compositions with the PRO of their choice. [Editor's note: Only one PRO is joined as a Writer. All PROs should be joined as a Publisher.]

Q: Does Hot Shoe Records release their catalog for streaming? If so, is Hot Shoe Records signed up with SoundExchange.com?

TONY: Hot Shoe Records is registered with both SoundExchange.com and Nielsen SoundScan.

Q: What service does Nielsen Soundscan perform for Hot Shoe Records and its artists?

TONY: Nielsen SoundScan tracks sales of music and music videos in the U.S. and Canada. To register with SoundScan you need both UPC and ISRC codes. To be considered for listing on the Billboard charts, an album needs to be registered with SoundScan.

Q: Does Hot Shoe Records help their artists sign up with SoundExchange.com so they can make money that way, too?

TONY: All Hot Shoe Records productions are registered by the label and any income from streaming is shared with the featured artist per their development agreement.

Q: Does Hot Shoe Records have their own branded International Standard Recording Code, or ISRC? If yes, how has that benefited the label? If not, why not?

TONY: An ISRC is not actually a brand per se, but is a unique identifier of the country of registration, label, release year, album ID, and track ID. The ISRC code starts with a unique label identifier which was assigned by RIAA to Hot Shoe Records through usisrc.org. The record company then generates the remainder of the code according to the international ISRC usage parameters. Every album and every track produced by Hot Shoe Records has an ISRC registered with RIAA, the designated ISRC agency for the U.S., and those ISRCs are included in each track and CD by embedding them during the mastering process.

[Editor's note: If you are serving as your own label, apply for your own unique identifier ISRC at usisrc.org]

Q: One thing that happens regularly with labels in other genres is the artist who manages to lay hands on a copy of their song and releases it as if it is theirs alone, when in fact they have somebody else acting as the "label". Then when the "label" goes to release it, they find the artist beat them to the punch and a whole lot of plans for monetizing go down the drain. How do you protect the earning potential of the songs and albums on your label?

TONY: Fortunately, this has not happened at Hot Shoe Records. But there is a reason for that. You see, a big part of the solution is taking care when choosing artists for the label. Also, having a written agreement for each album project is crucial. Hot Shoe Records is a label, not a production company, so we always retain copyright ownership of sound recordings. If all else fails, lawyer up.

Acknowledgements

All I wanted to do was write my songs and place them. To that end, I've spent a lot of time researching so that I could move forward productively. It quickly became clear that accurate information was not easily to be found — especially as it applied to the DIY/Indie. As a writer, I began sharing that information with other DIY/Indies and soon folks were saying "You should write a book about this." I did that in 2015 with *Navigating the New Music Business as a DIY & Indie — Coming Clean With the Down & Dirty.*

But my job as author is not only to pull together a set of information that would be practical, useful, and beneficial to those who have wondered how to make sense of a very complicated business, it is to keep that information updated and make it as easy as possible to quickly find what you need. I did that with this book.

But I did not do it alone.

Without the gracious and unselfish sharing of core sections of the music business by fellow DIY/Indies David LaMotte, Ken Bonfield, Marc Jackson, Lance Allen, and Tony Wasilewski, this book would have a limited benefit to you, the DIY/Indie reader.

So I thank these passionate, talented, and business-savvy men for each taking hours to be interviewed, answering even more questions in writing, and patiently walking me through their businesses, processes, challenges, and rewards as they have experienced the business.

As always, the keen editorial eye of Tom Whitfield polished the book as he "engineered and mastered" the manuscript. If there is a mistake here, it is because I ignored him.

Angela K. Durden
December 2018
In her production room where things creative happen.

BUSINESS BOOKS
by ANGELA K. DURDEN:
Nine Stupid Things People Do to Mess Up
Their Resumés (2000)

MEN! K.I.S.S. Your Resumé and Say Hello
to a Better Job (2013)
Also available as audio from Audible

LADIES! K.I.S.S. Your Resumé and Say
Hello to a Better Job (2013)

Opportunity Meets Motivation (2010)

Navigating the New Music Business as a
DIY and Indie: Coming Clean with the
Down and Dirty (2015)

CHILDREN'S BOOKS by AKD:
A Mike and His Grandpa Series:
Heroes Need Practice, Too! (2006)
The Balloon That Would Not Pop! (2012)

EXECUTIVE/DEVELOPMENTAL EDITOR for
I AM ISRAEL: Lions and Lambs of the Land
by Jedwin Smith (2018)

PUBLISHER at
WRITER for HIRE! Press
Second Bight Publishing
Blue Room Books

OTHER BOOKS by AKD:
Eloise Forgets How to Laugh (2010)
Twinkle, a memoir (2015)
First Time for Everything (2018)
Do Not Mistake This Smile (2018)

HUMOR
Dancing at the Waffle House
and other stories Neal Boorz wishes he had told
(2018)

Conversations in Hyperreality
and Other Thoughts Umberto Eco and Dave Barry Never Had
(Planned for mid-2019)

FICTION by DURDEN KELL:
Whitfield, Nebraska (2015)

TWO NOVEL SERIES
IN DEVELOPMENT:
The Case Files of Smith and Jones:
The Case of the Cotton Fiber Snuff Tape
The Case of the Cat-Loving Killer
The Case of the Angelic Assassin

The Dance Floor Wars:
Dispatches from the Front
Lucinda's People
Collisions
Life Cycle of a Fling

MUSIC BUSINESS SURVIVAL MANUAL
IMPRINT: SECOND BIGHT PUBLISHING
DECATUR, GEORGIA 30033

9 780985 462383

www.ingramcontent.com/pod-product-compliance
Lightning Source LLC
Chambersburg PA
CBHW060011050426
42448CB00012B/2709